Max Cleland is my special friend. His story is one you will never forget . . . this book will help you overcome setbacks and live life to the fullest . . . FANTASTIC!!

I keep several photos of Max Cleland on my office wall, next to my desk, to constantly remind me that I, too, can live life to the fullest, *regardless*. Now that he has written *Going for the Max! 12 Lessons Learned in Living Life to the Fullest*, I can take him with me wherever I go. Max Cleland is the right person to share this message. He is truly an inspiration; a National Treasure."

If maximizing our human potential is our goal, Senator Max Cleland is our coach and *Going for the Max!* is our manual.

GOING
FOR THE
MAX!

12 Principles for Living
Life to the Fullest

Max Cleland

BROADMAN
&HOLMAN
PUBLISHERS

Nashville, Tennessee

0-8054-2021-5

Published by Broadman & Holman Publishers, Nashville, Tennessee
Editorial Team: Vicki Crumpton, Janis Whipple, Kim Overcash
Typesetting: PerfecType, Nashville, Tennessee

Dewey Decimal Classification: 158
Subject Heading: Inspirational / Biography
Library of Congress Card Catalog Number: 99-31464

Every effort was made to secure complete information on all sources
for illustrations and quotes.

Unless otherwise noted, Scripture quotations are from the King
James Version. Also used are Holy Bible, New Living Translation,
copyright © 1996 by Tyndale Charitable Trust and New International
Version, copyright © 1973, 1978, 1984 by the International Bible Society.
All rights reserved.

Library of Congress Cataloging-in-Publication Data
Cleland, Max, 1942–
    Going for the max!: 12 lessons for living life to the fullest /
Max Cleland.
        p. cm.
    ISBN 0-8054-2021-5
    1. Self-actualization (Psychology) I. Title.
    BF637.S4C6   1999
    158.1—dc21

                                                              99-31464
                                                              CIP

1 2 3 4 5 03 02 01 00 99

DEDICATION

This book is dedicated to all of the many family members, friends, supporters, constituents, advisors, voters, and citizens who have encouraged me to go for the max in life. I appreciate you and am indebted to you more than you will ever know.

ACKNOWLEDGMENTS

The successful completion of any book is truly a team effort. I want to acknowledge the magnificent team that has brought this book to fruition. Special "thank-yous" go to:

Charlotte Hale, for her help, support, and deft execution of the idea for this book;

Lawrence Jordan, who as my book agent believed in me and the message I had to offer and lined me up with a marvelous publisher, Broadman & Holman;

Vicki Crumpton, my editor at Broadman & Holman who

took my calls late at night and tolerated "just one more change" in the manuscript;

Typists, Frances Lupton, Jennifer Wardrep, Frances Stewart, Carolina Loren, Karen Williams, Farrar Johnston, and Lena Kyle for their patience typing numerous versions of the manuscript and trying their best to read my handwriting;

Amy Kimball, for her superb handling of all the incredible details that come across the desk of a personal secretary to an author;

Wayne Howell, my Administrative Assistant, who has exercised the patience of Job and the wisdom of Solomon in leading and managing to perfection my Senate staff so I could finish this book;

Bill Chapman, the marvelous director of my Senate office in Georgia who has served as a mentor my entire life, who has gotten me out of more scrapes in my public career than the law allows for, and who has been to me the big brother I never had;

Dr. Lloyd Ogilvie, the Senate's inspiring chaplain, who has taught me the real meaning of Christian grace and joy and who has been a constant source of encouragement to me in every way, particularly in regard to this book;

Dr. John Eisold, the gifted Attending Physician of the Capitol, who has helped me deal with and overcome more health challenges than I can mention, who as a Navy Admiral always encourages me to never give up the ship;

My Senate staff members, who form the greatest team a Senator could ever hope to assemble, who have helped me walk through the mine fields of legislation, floor votes, and politics in our nation's capital and still survive;

Hugh and Juanita Cleland, who through their loving and selfless example have become their son's greatest heroes and who by their untiring support and encouragement not only enabled their son to be named "Max" but also enabled me to "Go for the Max" in life in every way;

Wally Amos, who has had more than his share of up and downs in his life but who has been a living example of how to "let go and let God";

Joey Reiman, my favorite "divergent thinker" who always inspires me to have my "reach exceed my grasp," to borrow Robert Browning's great phrase;

Steve Leeds, my honorary chief of staff, who always calms me down and helps me stay focused on my ultimate mission of doing a good job in the Senate;

Joe Sports, who introduced me to Georgia politics after I came back from Vietnam and who continues to help me stay on track;

Harry Stephens, who has proved time and again that real friendship lasts a lifetime;

Curtis Atkinson, who has exemplified the value of true loyalty in politics and in life;

And, to the Good Lord, who loves me anyway and who has given me, through the grace of God and the help of friends, the ability to go for the max in life;

I love you all!

CONTENTS

CONTENTS

FOREWORD

Years ago when I was the Pastor of the First Presbyterian Church of Hollywood, California, I received a letter from Max Cleland. After watching my television program *Let God Love You!* he wrote to encourage me. That began a friendship expressed in letters exchanged through the following years. We became prayer partners. I followed with intense interest and admiration his career in Georgia politics and the Veteran's Administration. The more I learned of his life and leadership, the more impressed I became. I realized that Max was not handicapped but "handicapable."

Several years later, I learned that Max was running for Sam Nunn's prestigious Senate seat. After his victory, it was a very special delight to welcome him to the Senate, where I was serving as chaplain.

I still can remember our joyous reunion. We almost disrupted a meeting where the new senators were being briefed on their duties. When Max was wheeled into the room, I hugged him and told him how happy I was that we would be serving our Lord, our beloved Nation, and the Senate together. With good-natured understanding, Majority Leader Senator Trent Lott said with a warm smile, "When the new senator of Georgia and the chaplain finish their greeting, we'll go on with the meeting!"

After Max was sworn in, my wife Mary Jane and I were privileged to join a group of over six hundred people who had come from Georgia to cheer the swearing in of their new senator. We all prayed for this immensely gifted leader and asked the Lord to bless him.

And He has! Max Cleland has had a wonderful impact on the life of the Senate. His leadership gifts and his contagiously positive spirit have inspired senators and staff alike. In the midst of the demanding, challenging, and sometimes enervating schedule of the Senate, Max brings pure joy.

Right from the beginning of his term, Senator Cleland became an active participant and leader in the Senate Bible studies, discussion groups, and the weekly prayer breakfast. Recently, he held a room full of senators in rapt attention as he spoke at the Wednesday morning prayer breakfast. And he seldom misses our senators' Bible study on Thursday noon. At one of these we studied Romans 8:28 in its more accurate translation of the Greek: "For we know that to those who love God, in all things God works together for good to those who are called according to His purpose." In the discussion, we worked out a motto for our fellowship: "Things don't work out; God works out things!" It's great to meet Max in the halls or as he is entering the Senate chamber. He gives me a "high five" and says with his customary enthusiasm, "God works out things!"

And He does. In all the ups and downs of life—with all our hopes and hurts—it has been a special privilege to share the delights—and difficulties—of life with Max as his friend and chaplain. We've laughed and cried together and shared life's joys and sorrows.

Max is one of my wife's favorite senators. They too have a super friendship. It's fun when we all can break bread together in the Senate Dining Room or take in a movie.

Max Cleland is a remarkable human being. He is a disciple of our Lord who lives on the growing edge. His sharp mind is filled with insight and inspiration from his commitment to keep on reading, learning, and storing up quotable quotes. He is a very capable political leader. Most of all, his commitment to our Lord is expressed in patriotism. Max loves America and serves in the Senate with the same unswerving dedication he did in Vietnam.

All that I've said about the senator has been to lead up to this: I want to take your hand and place it in Max's (his strong left hand; his right hand and legs were blown off by a grenade in Vietnam). I want you to know each other and enjoy a friendship. This book is like a personal conversation with this great American and man of God. In it he shares twelve of the most important discoveries of his life. Each chapter is power-packed and filled with stories, anecdotes, and stunning quotes that will keep you turning the pages as you read on with amazement at what Max Cleland has learned from the adventure of living life to the fullest.

Here is a powerful, positive book that will bring new gusto to your life. Reading it, you will want to go for the max. And why not?

> Dr. Lloyd John Ogilvie
> 61st United States Senate Chaplain
> Washington, D.C.

INTRODUCTION

"*Always be able to look back and say,
'At least I didn't lead no humdrum life.'*"

—*Forrest Gump*

Winston Churchill, one of my favorite heroic figures of the twentieth century, once observed that he could enjoy life more because he knew the deprivation of being in the trenches. After a military debacle in World War I which cost Churchill his job as First Lord of the Admiralty, Churchill was indeed sent to the trenches. He saw the devastation and tragedy of the loss of human life in World War I up close and in a very personal way.

I've spent some time in the trenches myself. I have seen and experienced the tragedy and loss of human life in the Vietnam War. In 1968, a grenade explosion cost me both legs and my right arm. Since then I've known the frustration of dealing with a physical disability. I am well-acquainted with the sorrow of defeat and the sting of personal failure and rejection. I have known the suffering of physical illness and the sadness of despair. But that actually causes me to want to live life even more, not less.

As I recovered from my wounds in Vietnam, my first objective was to get back on my feet, so to speak, and return to society as a contributing human being. I told that story in my first book, *Strong at the Broken Places*. The phrase, "strong at the broken places," comes from a line in Ernest Hemingway's magnificent novel based on his experiences in World War I, *A Farewell to Arms*. The quote, one of my favorites, is this: "The world breaks everyone, and afterward, many are strong at the broken places."

What do we do after we recover from whatever it is that has set us back? I think we set new goals. I think we sink our roots deeper into our own soul and find out more of who we are and what God wants us to be. Invariably, when I have done that in my own life, the message comes back strong and clear time after time: "Go for the max! Be all you can be! Shoot your best shot! Live life to the fullest!"

That is what this book is all about. It deals with going for the "max" in life. It is all about living life to the fullest. The ancient Greeks called this attitude *kleos*. For the Greeks, living life to the fullest meant living a life worthy of praise. For the Chinese, the word is *li*. It is the Chinese description for a true passion for living.

By whatever name it is called, living life to the fullest is something I believe we all want to accomplish and we were all born to do. My Bible tells me that our Creator designed us to live life "more abundantly."

It is my experience that with God's help and with the help of good friends, we can do that. There are some fundamental lessons, though, I've learned about going for the max in my life. I think they apply to all of us. I've identified twelve of them. These "lessons learned" are the subject of this book. They have played a critical role in enabling me to bounce back from tragedy and move on to live the life of my dreams. They have helped me go for the max in my life. I hope they help you do the same!

Max Cleland
United States Senator
Washington, D.C.

1

LIFE IS A DARING ADVENTURE

"Life is either a daring adventure or nothing.
To keep our faces toward change, and behave like free spirits in
the presence of fate is strength undefeatable!"

—Helen Keller

W hat could be worse than losing your sight?" someone once asked Helen Keller, who had lost her eyesight and hearing after an early childhood illness.

"Losing your vision," she replied. Helen Keller had learned that despite disabilities or all else that goes against us in life, if we keep our vision and live life as a daring adventure, our most cherished dreams can come true.

Rudyard Kipling, the famous British poet, described such daring:

"If you can make one heap of all your winnings,

And risk it all on one turn of pitch-and-toss,

And lose, and start again at your beginnings

And never breathe a word about your loss . . ."

If you dare to do those things, the Kipling poem concludes, "Yours is the earth and everything that's in it. . . ."

In the movie *Tin Cup*, Kevin Costner portrays a washed-up former college golf star who has become reduced to working for a driving range in a nondescript Texas border town. Nearly destitute, he possesses none of the attributes of a winner except for one strong, overriding belief. There are certain "defining moments" in life, the golfer tells us, when you must risk it all.

The story climaxes with the golfer chasing his "impossible" personal dream—challenging himself to play in the U.S. Open and achieve his vision of becoming a golf pro. His defining moment arrives with the shot that can bring him a tie for the

> *"Tentative efforts lead to tentative outcomes. Therefore, give yourself fully to your endeavors. Decide to construct your character through excellent actions and determine to pay the price of a worthy goal. The trials you encounter will introduce you to your strengths. Remain steadfast . . . and one day you will build something that endures: something worthy of your potential."*
>
> *—Epictetus*

lead, but he chooses instead to go for the win . . . and promptly plops the ball into the water hazard. He tries again but with the same sickening result. Again and again the golfer takes the daring approach, deliberately choosing to risk failure rather than take the safe route and "lay up" on the green.

At last, on his final chance, his last ball, he hits the ball all the way in the hole! Costner's character dared to go for it all and so achieved far more than he ever dreamed he could.

The film motivates me. I can identify with both sides of Costner's hero—the loser who no longer sees himself as someone capable of succeeding, and the magnificent human being who seizes the moment when he dares to go for the max and win it all! The test for me is to minimize my tendency to think of myself as a loser and maximize my tendency to think of myself as a winner.

I have to challenge myself constantly not to lose my vision about what I can become. I have to remind myself constantly that life is a daring adventure—or nothing!

When we fail, we temporarily lose my vision of life as a daring adventure. But General George S. Patton Jr. said it very well: "Success is how high you bounce after you hit bottom." Perhaps we can't help hitting bottom, but we shouldn't forget to remind ourselves of how high we can bounce!

LOVE THE LITTLE THINGS

I hope that I will never lose my vision of life as a daring adventure. Former U.S. Supreme Court Justice Arthur Goldberg once referred to the process of progress as coming "inch by agonizing inch." To me that presents the challenge to inch toward the goal I can only feel, and maybe not see clearly. Whenever I have lost my vision, I've concentrated on doing the little things.

Mother Teresa, the tiny, frail Roman Catholic nun who chose to serve the poorest of the poor, radiated uncommon joy and exuberance for life. Many of the world's most powerful and respected persons revered her for her simple, unselfish goodness. Many asked for the secret of her great accomplishments. Her answer was simple: "There are no great things; just little things done with great love."

Great people know that a great life is not merely a pull-yourself-up-by-your-bootstraps operation. I like an interview Mother Teresa had once:

Question: "Mother Teresa, when you talk to God, what do you say?"

Answer: "I don't say anything. I just listen."

Question: "Mother Teresa, when God talks to you, what does He say?"

Answer: "He doesn't say anything. He just listens."

In his final speech to the U.S. Congress, Senator Hubert Humphrey talked about the little things and the little people. He stated that the moral test of government is "how it treats those in the dawn of life, the children; those in the twilight of life, the elderly; and those in the shadows of life, the disabled." I can identify with the little people. I am one.

Because of my own personal struggle to become "strong at the broken places," I can comprehend something of the struggle of others who need and desire wholeness in their lives. This is one reason I chose to enter politics, to serve the little people. I try to do it with great love.

> "Go not where the path may lead.
> Go instead where no man has gone before
> and blaze a new trail."
>
> —Ralph Waldo Emerson

Admiral "Bull" Halsey, a tough old salt in the U.S. Navy during the Second World War, was fond of telling the Navy servicemen who were under his command in the South Pacific: "There are no great men; just great challenges ordinary men like you and I must face." I like that. I may not always feel "great," but by focusing on the "little things" and the "little people," I can keep my eye on great challenges.

> *"God is in the details"*
> —*Friedrich Nietzsche*

Golda Meir, the famed former prime minister of Israel, was once asked to describe the people of her nation. She replied, "They are ordinary people doing extraordinary things the best way they can." What a marvelous thing to be said of any of us.

Focusing on the little things has great practical value. First, it helps us become more disciplined. There is a proverb which says: "If you are washing dishes, wash dishes." Focusing on the little things gives us the discipline to concentrate on what we are doing at the time we are doing it. Doing little things well is how we build the strongest foundation for a successful life.

There's a story about a man who visited a site where a beautiful cathedral was being constructed. The visitor asked one worker what he was doing. He said, "Lifting bricks." He asked another worker what he was doing. He replied, "Building a cathedral." If we do the little things, they will help us build the cathedral of our lives.

Dr. Martin Luther King Jr., one of my personal heroes, understood the value of doing the little things. He realized that though we may not be equal in abilities, backgrounds, or even the choices we make, we can all concentrate on the little things in an excellent way. He once wrote, "If you are a street sweeper, sweep the streets like Beethoven wrote music, like Shakespeare wrote poetry and like Rembrandt painted pictures. Sweep the streets so well that when you pass away, all the hosts of heaven and earth will say, 'Here was a street sweeper who did his job well!'"[1]

Mahatma Gandhi, the great nonviolent leader for India's independence, inspired Dr. King. Gandhi disciplined himself to focus on little things every day. He was a weaver of cloth. His feet provided the mechanical power for the loom. His hands were used for the repetitious task of weaving the thread. What might have seemed a waste of time for a world leader was actually part of Gandhi's view of success. His weaving, he said, helped him focus on the little things that were important to him. It helped him keep in touch with life, with living, and with the world around him.

Winston Churchill, according to his aides, frustrated his subordinates with constant memos asking minute questions about the details of World War II. His staff called the memos "the prime minister's prayers" because they always started with the phrase, "Pray tell me why . . . ?"

Great leaders are people like you and me. They are ordinary citizens, but they focus on the little things and the little people, relate to them in an extraordinary way, and they try to live life as a daring adventure.

While on active duty in the U.S. Army, General Colin Powell used to tell his young officers not to worry about promotions. "Take care of your men and your mission," he said. "Your promotions and your career will take care of themselves."

In doing what we can do, focusing on the little things and the little people, and in doing things with great love, we can live life as a daring adventure beyond our wildest dreams.

> *"You miss 100 percent of the shots you never take."*
> —Wayne Gretzky

One dream I had was to go into politics after my service in the military. That dream led to one of the most daring acts of my life. I ran for and won a race for the United States Senate. On January 7, 1997, I was sworn into office. There are no words to describe the thoughts and emotions which flooded over me on that unforgettable day.

I remember moving in front of Al Gore, Vice President of the United States and the Senate's presiding officer, flanked by Senator Sam Nunn, Georgia's outgoing senior senator, and Senator Paul Coverdell, our junior senator, who served as my honorary escorts. The Vice President asked the small group of incoming U.S. senators to raise their right hands to take the oath. Then he glanced at me: "Or your left hand, as the case may be," he muttered.

When Vice President Gore administered the oath of office to me as a U.S. senator in 1997 and I repeated his words, my memory took me back. I had taken a similar oath as a young lieutenant upon being commissioned in the United States Army in June 1964. I took an oath again on March 2, 1977, upon beginning my work as head of the U.S. Veterans Administration under President Jimmy Carter. Now, on this third occasion of taking that same oath, I raised my left hand and placed the stump of my right hand on my Bible. This was a special Bible. It was the one I read as a boy growing up in Lithonia, Georgia. It was the same Bible my dad carried in his duffel bag when he was a young sailor with the U.S. Navy, stationed at Pearl Harbor during World War II. He had given me that Bible to take with me to Vietnam.

When I first went to Washington as a student during the 1960s, I had dared to dream of some day becoming involved in politics. An eminent psychologist, Erick Erickson, once said that parents who are not afraid to die can raise children who are not afraid to live. I was not afraid to live! I ultimately was not afraid to run for public office. In 1996, I had my defining moment. I took my shot at the U.S. Senate and made a hole-in-one. I'm living proof that your dreams can come true if you live life as a daring adventure!

RISK
CHANGING

"Change is good. You go first."

—*Dilbert cartoon*

W e cannot become what we need to be by remaining what we are," observed Max DePree.

Thomas Carlyle put it another way when he wrote, "Change indeed is painful, yet ever needful."

I've certainly found that true in my life. After being sworn in to the U.S. Senate in 1997, I had attained a great dream in my life . . . that of sitting in the United States Congress. Running for office, though, had taken a toll on me physically. I was grossly overweight, sleeping poorly, and was not at my peak performance. I was not maxing out my life.

Over the past couple of years I've had to drastically change the way I eat, sleep, and exercise. I've had to regulate my intake of carbohydrates, get to bed at a decent hour, and adopt a regimen which gives me the stamina to do my job. To change the way I eat, sleep, and exercise was one of the most difficult challenges I've ever faced. It's been painful. I still slip back into old patterns and old habits occasionally. Nevertheless, I am learning to change!

> *"Don't look at the sudden loss of a habit or way of life as the end of the road; see it instead as only a bend in the road that will open up all sorts of interesting possibilities and new experiences."*
> —*Mary Pickford*

> *"I find that the great thing in this world*
> *is not where we stand, as in what*
> *direction we are moving."*
> —*Oliver Wendell Holmes*

IT TAKES GUTS TO LEAVE THE RUTS

Dr. Robert Schuller has a line I like: "It takes guts to leave the ruts." Do I agree with that! Often I wait until a crisis is upon me before I change. In the Chinese language, the word crisis is written in two characters: one means "danger," the other means "opportunity." Many times I have to confront the danger before I can take advantage of the opportunity.

I like the story of home-run king Mark McGuire. McGuire said he had a rough past life. "I wasn't a very secure person," he related. "I could never face the truth. I always ran from it. It's like sometimes I look back at myself in those days and think, 'Who was I?'"

Today McGuire is a new man. According to a *Sports Illustrated* story, "His acts of graciousness have done as much for baseball as his athletic prowess. Welcoming his competitor, Sammy Sosa, into his home-run race, McGuire incorporated some of Sosa's gestures in his home run to honor him. When he hit the sixty-second homer, McGuire jumped the box seat railing to hug Roger Maris's six grown children, trying to make them feel included in the experience, rather than excluded."

The article concludes, "Not only has the Mark McGuire of 1998 given America something to cheer about, he has shown us it's never too late to change."

Dr. Charles Allen, a beloved Methodist minister, author, and my friend, once wrote: "Valleys are for moving through, not wallowing in." Dr. Allen was referring to King David, the Old Testament psalmist, who knew about the valleys of life. David, whom the Bible describes as "a man after God's own heart," experienced defeat, embarrassment, hurt, ridicule, pain, and tragedy. In the Twenty-third Psalm, David told of "the valley of the shadow of death." Interestingly, I think it was not death, but the *shadow* of death, which unnerved the warrior king. I can identify with David. Shadows. Fears. Apparitions. Apprehensions. Guilt. Sorrow. Regret. I recognize each of these shadows. They so often have paralyzed me and prevented me from going for the max in my life.

I'm encouraged, though. The Old Testament points a way out of the valley. "Yea, through I walk *through* the valley of the shadow of death . . ." David did not camp out in the valley; he kept on moving!

> *"It is better by noble boldness to run the risk of being subject to half of the evils we anticipate than to remain in cowardly listlessness for fear of what may happen."*
>
> —*Herodotus*

Robert Louis Stevenson once observed, "Saints are sinners who keep on trying." To escape a valley or rut, keep on trying, keep on moving *through* the valley.

David realized that it is in our deadening rut, or our deepest valley of heartache and despair, that we can learn life's most magnificent truth: *God is with us.* David discovered, "For thou art with me. Thy rod and thy

> *"Look abroad at nature's range; Nature's mighty power is change."*
> —*Robert Burns*

staff, they comfort me." David believed God was with him in any change he had to go through. Wow! That inspires me. That helps me to keep on moving in my daily struggle to go for the max in life!

VALLEYS ARE TEMPORARY

President Abraham Lincoln once told an interesting story to his fellow citizens of Springfield, Illinois. Lincoln said a monarch of the East once asked his wise men to tell him one precept which always would be true. The wise men conferred, then answered: "This too shall pass."

The story is particularly poignant. Lincoln then boarded a train for Washington, D.C., where he knew he must attempt to lead a divided nation through the agonies of the Civil War. For Lincoln, those days of change—national change—must have seemed agonizingly slow. It does help us to realize that change and turmoil won't always be around. It helps me to know such days will pass.

SPRINGBOARDS TO EXHILARATING CHANGE

As tough as they are to endure, I believe valleys, ruts, and personal trials actually help us to go for the max in life—if we learn to change. As Helen Keller wrote, "The mountaintops of our world would not be nearly so wonderful if there were no dark valleys to traverse."

> *"Very often a change of self is needed more than a change of scene."*
> —*Arthur C. Benson*

Life happens. We must learn to change or be stuck in our ruts forever. If we do change, joy and self-fulfillment can be the exhilarating result! We can go for the max if we risk changing!

PREPARE YOURSELF TO WIN

"Chance favors the prepared mind."

—*Louis Pasteur*

Winston Churchill once pointed out:

> "To all of us comes that moment in life when we are literally tapped on the shoulder to do a very special thing unique to ourselves and our talents. What a pity if that moment finds us unprepared."

Churchill ought to have known. The man who William Manchester calls "the last lion" spent virtually his entire life *preparing* for his great role as leader of Great Britain in World War II.

Abraham Lincoln understood the value of preparing himself for a historic role. "I will prepare myself and mayhap my chance will come," said Lincoln.

Thomas Jefferson had his own view of preparation. He said he was a great believer in luck: the harder he worked, the more he had of it.

If this is the way great leaders look at the value of preparation, then we must prepare ourselves also!

I've discovered it's not an easy or quick task to prepare oneself. It can take years. But we can do it!

I like what Bobby Knight, the great basketball coach of the University of Indiana, has to say about the value of preparation. "A lot of people have the will to win," Coach Knight points out, "but not many have the will to prepare to win."

PRACTICE, PRACTICE, AND MORE PRACTICE

Not long ago in my home state of Georgia, a young man wanted to go out for the high school football team. He was slow and awkward, not very good in spring football practice.

"Go home and develop yourself," his coach advised him.

"How?" the young man asked.

"The best way to get stronger is by doing push-ups, sit-ups, and sprints."

In late August, preseason football practice began. The coach immediately noticed something new about the backfield's offense. A young man seemed to dominate the game. When he carried the ball, things happened. The coach approached the tall, skinny youngster and asked his name. "I'm the kid who asked you how to get stronger and faster," the boy replied.

"What did you do?" the coach asked in disbelief.

"What you told me, sir."

"And what was that?"

"Push-ups, sit-ups, and sprints," the young athlete replied.

"That's all?" the astonished coach persisted.

"Yes sir," the young man said, "I prepared myself just the way you told me to do."

"What's your name, son?" the coach asked.

"Sir, I'm Herschel Walker," the future sports hero announced.

■ ■ ■

I have visited with Herschel Walker on many occasions. He is an incredible gentleman and athlete. Before his days in professional football, he led his high school to the Georgia state championship. He was the highly recruited tailback and freshman legend at the University of Georgia, and led the Georgia Bulldogs to the national championship in 1980 during his first season on the team.

This quiet, superbly fit man impresses me. The Herschel Walker story captures my imagination.

Herschel's football career started in high school on those hot, muggy south Georgia nights in which a tired youngster made himself *run* home from football practice. As he would approach the most difficult part of the road leading to his house in rural Johnson County, Georgia, Herschel would stop to tie a tire behind his back. Then he would *sprint* more than one hundred yards before he allowed himself to collapse onto the porch steps and call it a day.

Herschel Walker exemplifies the *will to prepare* to win. That will to prepare created one of the fastest, most powerful tailbacks ever in college football. He won the prestigious Heisman Trophy in only his third college season.

Walker's preparation for winning never stops. He *still* does sit-ups, push-ups, and sprints. The will to prepare, and to keep on preparing, is one of the keys to Herschel Walker's success.

■　　■　　■

> *"Nature cannot be tricked or cheated. She will give up to you the object of your struggles only after you have paid her price."*
>
> —*Napoleon Hill*

Another friend who became a true champion is Evander Holyfield. As a youth in an Atlanta elementary school, Evander was taken to the downtown Boy's Club, a place where inner-city kids can go for recreation and fun. Here Evander discovered the world of boxing. In fact, when an adult asked him who he was, the boy answered, "I'm Evander Holyfield and I'm a boxer." Holyfield envisioned himself as a champion even as a youngster. But many years of intense preparation would come before he could claim his first title.

In 1984, Evander Holyfield was one of many American youths hoping to make it to the 1984 Olympic Games. To add to his pressures, the young man needed a car. Evander entered a dealership in Morrow, a town just south of Atlanta. He knew no one at the business, but as he was asking about buying a car he ran across the owner of the dealership, Ken Sanders.

Evander's dignity, sincerity, and purpose impressed Sanders. He saw something special in the young man, took a chance, and sold Holyfield a car. That act of trust would hold great consequences for both men. A few nights later, Sanders

> *"If you have built castles in the air, you need not be lost; that is where they should be. Now put foundations under them."*
>
> —Henry David Thoreau

received a telephone call from Evander. It became a man-to-man conversation. A bond of respect had been forged during the automobile purchase. Evander needed a mentor, a friend . . . someone who would listen.

That evening, Holyfield told Sanders he had a shot at making the United States Olympic boxing team. The rules stipulated that he would have to defeat two strong opponents on two successive nights in order to make the team. Evander told Sanders he wasn't sure he could do it.

Sanders encouraged the young man not to give up. "You can do it, Evander," his new friend insisted. That conversation turned the tide. Evander won both events. He became part of the 1984 Olympics. Another young man who, by the way, did *not* make the team was a youthful boxer named Mike Tyson. I truly believe that later in their careers, when Evander and Tyson squared off, Evander may have been one of the few people in the world who really thought he could beat Tyson in their celebrated match. I believe he must have drawn strength from knowing he had survived those long-ago Olympic trials and Tyson had not.

Few people know that before becoming an Olympic champion, however, Evander Holyfield had a job pumping gas at an airport. While pumping gas, he was also pumping himself into shape. Young as he was, he was preparing himself to go for the max! During his breaks, Evander ducked into nearby hangars where he could exercise. Those brief, intense workouts fueled his powerful will to win.

When Evander turned pro, he hired Ken Sanders as his first professional manager. Holyfield went on to become the heavyweight champion of the world. He won the coveted title *three times*. Only one other man in the history of boxing—the great Muhammad Ali—has accomplished such a feat.

WINNING HABITS AND MIND-SETS

Early on, I learned the value of preparing myself to be successful. One lesson took place on October 18, 1965, when I reported for duty at Fort Gordon, Georgia, as a twenty-two-year-old second lieutenant in the U.S. Army.

After our first week of training, Col. Bob Pearle, our commander, held a reception for young lieutenants like me who were just entering the army.

We all looked up to Colonel Pearle as an exceptional man who had distinguished himself in tank battles in World War II. We instantly sensed his fitness to lead. When he spoke, we listened.

I shall always remember our first meeting with Colonel Pearle. He called all of us by our first names. He even mentioned our hometowns! Imagine how impressed we were at his preparing to lead us. When a busy man makes the effort to memorize personal information about fifty junior officers, his example teaches those men far more than mere lectures can do.

Colonel Pearle once gave me good advice. "Remember, lieutenant," he stated, "the army is ninety percent hard work, nine percent adventure, and one percent pure panic." His message was pointed. Preparation requires hard work, yet it remains absolutely essential to winning battles in war or in life. The unspoken, additional message in his advice came through loud and clear. The better the preparation, the less the panic. I took his teaching to heart.

Former President Jimmy Carter served in the U.S. Navy under Admiral Hyman Rickover, founder of the U.S. Navy submarine program. Carter recalls receiving the same sort of advice from his famous commander. "The more you sweat in peacetime, the less you bleed in war," Rickover used to say. Carter recounted many of the lessons he learned from Admiral Rickover about being willing to prepare in a best-selling book

> *Know ye not that they which run in a race*
> *run all, but one receiveth the prize?*
> *So run, that ye may obtain.*
> —*1 Corinthians 9:24*

entitled *Why Not the Best?* He credits many of those lessons as preparing him to become President of the United States.

PREPARING FOR OPPORTUNITY

Another lesson in the value of preparing myself was when my mother enrolled me as a six-year-old in piano lessons. I hated them. I avoided practice, forgot my practice book (how convenient), and would blank out at recitals. But I practiced nevertheless. Later, it paid off.

I learned to play the trumpet and the French horn. In fact, I was selected for the high school band while in the fifth grade. Those countless hours of practice ultimately repaid me many times over with a lifelong love and appreciation for music.

Where I really learned to sweat and prepare myself, however, was in sports. I loved all sports. I loved to win. Through sports, a good deal of my personal confidence and positive self-image as a young man was formed. Competitive sports taught me very early that hard work and preparation make an enormous difference in a game's outcome, especially in the game of life.

I was the first in my high school class to get an athletic letter. I earned the letter in the ninth grade for playing third base on the varsity baseball team. I lettered in baseball four years in a row.

Then there was swimming. I earned a Red Cross Junior Life Saving Certificate and in swim meets was undefeated in the backstroke.

In tennis singles, I won my city's championship my senior year and placed second in the state.

But basketball was my sports passion. I identified with Jerry West, legendary player for the Los Angeles Lakers. His brother had been killed in the Korean Conflict. Jerry said he learned how to shoot basketball because it was a game you could play by yourself. As an only child, I was by myself a lot. A basketball was my constant companion. Rain or shine, I'd shoot all year long. During the off season, I'd shoot wads of paper into trash baskets. I put up a small goal in my basement and "dunked it" constantly. Year after year, I had a ball of some kind in my hand, playing with it, dribbling it, shooting it.

> *"If I do not practice one day, God knows it.*
> *If I do not practice the next, God and I know*
> *it. If I do not practice the third day,*
> *the entire world knows it."*
>
> —*Ignace Jan Paderewski*

I became the tallest guy in my class at six feet two inches. A basketball and I seemed to be made for each other. Offense was my thing. I loved to put points on the board. Looking back, I realize I was willing to put in that ninety percent hard work Colonel Pearle talked about for the adventure of playing the game. I prepared myself to go for the max!

OTHER LESSONS LEARNED

One of the people who taught me sports and the value of practice was Edgar Abbott, my backyard school chum. Edgar was two years older than I and was a born teacher and coach. He would let me win at basketball just enough to keep me encouraged, but he could beat me when he really wanted to. Whether in tennis, baseball, football, or especially in basketball, Edgar made me stretch.

Edgar taught me to strive beyond what I thought I could do. He taught me to play and practice until I couldn't stand up. I sweated until I thought I would die, but Edgar led me to learn. I learned how to prepare myself to go for the max!

Edgar Abbott has been a band director at Ft. Knox High School in Kentucky, now, for more than thirty years. He has spent an entire career coaching and teaching others how to go for the max too. He is one of my favorite heroes in my life.

■　■　■

Then came the year I learned about losing. As a tenth-grader selected for the basketball team, I played my heart out. Yet the team won only one ball game all year—one win and nineteen losses! I was not used to losing. I wondered what had gone wrong.

Coach Ralph McReynolds, a newcomer coach that year just as I was a newcomer player, reassured me. "Keep working.

We'll get 'em next year," he said. I really believed that. I took basketball practice more seriously than ever. I shot basketball in the rain and the cold. I practiced, practiced, and practiced.

During the next season, I substituted one night as forward for a sick teammate. I shot sixteen points that game. I won a steady slot at forward. I often think back to the fact that if I had given up during the year we had our losing season and not continued to prepare myself for the winning season, I would have missed out on a great deal.

Preparing myself is one of the important lessons I have learned in going for the max. Later, such dedication to preparation would come in handy as I faced the toughest challenge of my life—making a comeback after the loss of both my legs and my shooting arm. The lessons I learned in hard work, preparation, patience, and practice as a boy paid off in later years as I attempted to become "strong at the broken places."

> *"There is no great achievement that is not the result of patience, working, and waiting."*
> —*Josiah Holland*

4

YOU
GOTTA
BELIEVE

"All things are possible to one who believes."

—*St. Bernard of Clairvaux*

T he year was 1969. The New York Mets baseball team was low in the standings in midsummer. It seemed impossible to fight back to first place. However, the team slowly began to come alive. In the fall, they caught fire! Tug McGraw, a pitcher for the Mets, articulated a saying that caught on among his teammates: "You gotta believe."

Believe they did. The Mets went on to win the World Series that year.

Whatever we want in life, we've gotta believe it, if it's going to happen. Hugh Cleland, my father, taught me that lesson very early in my life. A successful salesman for more than sixty years, Daddy imparted his success secret to me: "If I believe in something, I can sell it!"

My mother and father have lived lives that demonstrate the power of belief: belief in yourself, in God, in hard work, in worthwhile goals, in high objectives, in our nation, and the importance of serving others.

Growing up among people of faith convinces me, "You gotta believe!" if you want to go for the max!

PLANTING THE SEED OF FAITH

There is great power in belief. It is the power of the seed. As the Bible says, the seed need not be big—in fact, it can be quite small—but it does have to be planted. A seed has great possibilities!

Learning how to plant seeds of faith leads to some great adventures. As Dr. Robert Schuller says, "Any fool can count the number of seeds in an apple. Only God can count the number of apples in a seed." It's exciting to plant a seed without knowing how many apples we'll get. With apologies to Forrest Gump, life is far more than "a box of chocolates." Life can become the daring adventure it is supposed to become when we plant seeds of faith—particularly in our mind.

Herschel Walker once explained the power of his mind in achieving his exceptional physical strength. He stated, "My mind is the general. My body is the army."

Napoleon Bonaparte, the great French general, understood the power of the mind and of faith in winning battles. Napoleon once pointed out that "imagination rules the world." He stated that once a battle was begun, however, his role as leader was to become a "purveyor of hope."

Winston Churchill also understood that. He once observed, "The empires of the future are the empires of the mind." A mind full of faith can build and conquer empires.

Another Napoleon, Napoleon Hill, once studied successful people. In his book, *Laws of Success,* published in the 1930s, he conveyed his findings that belief plays a key role in determining a person's success. Hill's observations underscore the power of the human mind. "What you can conceive and believe, you can achieve," he wrote.

> *"Faith is the bird that feels the light and sings when the dawn is still dark."*
>
> —*Rabindranath Tagore*

Faith and belief have fascinated thinkers, writers, scientists, and others throughout the ages. Germany's great poet, Goethe, put it this way: "Whatever you dream you can, begin it; boldness has genius, power and magic in it."

The Bible, of course, holds many towering truths about faith. One verse I like states it plainly: "According to your faith be it unto you" (Matt. 9:29). If we can conceive it and believe it, God will help us achieve it.

Henry David Thoreau wrote that once a person has made up his mind about what he wants, he or she will meet with success "unexpected in common hours." The American inventor, Alexander Graham Bell, concurred. Commenting about the power of faith, Bell stated, "Where this power comes from I do not know. I just know that it exists!"

> *"Faith is believing in that in which you have not seen.*
> *The reward of faith is seeing that in which you have believed."*
>
> —*St. Augustine*

If I want something to happen, I've found I must plant the seed of that future experience deep in my mind. I must water that seed of faith. I must follow Andrew Carnegie's advice to "place all your eggs in one basket, then watch that basket!" I've learned to plant my seeds of faith, then watch them grow into reality.

■   ■   ■

The power of belief was reinforced for me in 1969 by an experience I had while struggling to learn how to walk on artificial limbs. A Disabled American Veterans chapter in New York City enlisted some of us amputees from Walter Reed and the V.A. hospital in Washington, D.C. to come to the Big Apple for a good time.

At one of the events on that New York trip, something amazing happened. I noticed a smiling, well-dressed man enter the room with a lovely lady on his arm. Immediately people around me started trying to get my attention.

"That's Sammy Neuzoff," they whispered, as the gentleman walked around to me.

"He has no legs and no knees," the whisperers told me. A shock ran through me. *This man was just like me . . . .*

But there he was, walking . . . on artificial limbs. Sammy Neuzoff, a World War II veteran, looked happy, relaxed, normal, . . . *and he was walking.* That moment marked a turning point in my rehabilitation. For the first time since my injury, I saw with my own eyes that success could be achieved. *If Sammy could do it, I could do it,* I told myself.

I cannot describe the power of that realization. For the first time since I had been wounded, I really believed I would walk on artificial limbs. From that point on, I would not accept rejection!

Later that year I walked out of the V.A. hospital in Washington, D.C., on my own artificial limbs. Not many people thought I could do it, and few encouraged me to try. However, everyone helped me, and everyone cheered my efforts. Learning to use new legs had been my goal, my idea, and I stuck with it until I won the victory. A few years later I decided to abandon them. They were too cumbersome and actually slowed me down. I could get more places more easily in a wheelchair. I decided to "run" for politics in a wheelchair rather than to "walk" on artificial legs. But my experience about the trial of learning to walk on artificial limbs reinforced my belief in the power of belief itself. If you are going for the max in life, you gotta believe.

I've found that faith needs to be strengthened continually. We are not perfect. Our faith lags and drags from time to time. This is where our belief in the goodness of God and the love of our friends makes a tremendous difference.

I find my greatest challenge is keeping faith in myself! A psychologist friend offered an interesting solution to those days when you wake up feeling nothing good is going to happen.

> *"I tell you the truth, if you have faith as small as a mustard seed, you can say to this mountain 'Move from here to there' and it will move. Nothing will be impossible for you."*
>
> —*Matthew 17:20–21*, NIV

"Allow some good things into your life," he suggested. "Treat yourself with the utmost respect. Do little things for yourself, the kind of nice small gestures you'd make toward a friend in the same circumstances."

One morning, feeling down on myself, I decided to try this advice. I'd go for the max. First, I took a wonderful warm shower. I splashed on my favorite after-shave lotion. I put on one of my best shirts and a really great tie.

After just an hour of being good to myself, I had a completely different picture of the world . . . and myself too! I understood the principle behind my friend's prescription: when I neglect myself because I am too rushed, too busy, or too distracted, I run out of gas. I lose connections with myself, my friends, and my Creator. My faith gauge starts pointing to empty. I have to slow down and be good to myself.

I believe most of us travel in a condition of low self-esteem. This is the twentieth century's bubonic plague. It is a disease so widespread that we find it everywhere. It compromises our ability to accomplish great things. It prevents us from living life as a daring adventure. It saps our ability to go for the max in life.

These days the importance of a healthy self-esteem is being recognized for the powerful force it truly is. As Dr. Schuller says, "The me I see is the me I'll be." I agree with that. I believe there's a direct correlation between *how* we see ourselves and *what* we can accomplish in life.

I have to remind myself to believe, not just in my Creator, but in what my Creator created—me. I need to constantly remind myself, "God don't make no junk."

I have discovered that believing is much more than wishful thinking. It is much more than just hanging your life on a wing and a prayer. Faith cannot be seen, but the *outcome* of faith *can* be seen. Although real faith works that way—we must *believe* it in order to *see* it—it's always a great inspiration for me to see how the power of faith works in the lives of others.

I believe God works in mysterious ways to bring certain people into our lives to enhance our faith. These people are living faith builders. They help us see in them what we long to *believe* in us!

FAITH THAT MOVES MOUNTAINS

Keeping the faith is difficult. When I am hurt, my self-confidence is the first thing to go. I can remember days and months after I was wounded when I avoided looking into the mirror. The sight of my physical appearance was too much for me to bear. Such startling feedback so early after my injury depleted my strength and sapped my faith.

Whenever I would look into a mirror after I was wounded, I used to feel lower than a worm. But after a while, at least I began to feel better! As time went on, every basic instinct I possessed began to tell me I was not a worm. I began to feel and believe I was a human being meant to go for the max!

When we do go for the max in our lives, there is a light and life around us that glows. We have become believers: in ourselves, our Creator, our goals, our purpose, and our individual destinies. We become "children of light," in theologian Reinhold Neibuhr's great phrase. Through faith, through belief, we move from darkness into the light, from the seen to the unseen. As Ralph Waldo Emerson so beautifully expressed it: "All that I have seen causes me to trust the Creator with all I have not seen."

> *"They can conquer who believe they can."*
> —Ralph Waldo Emerson

FAITH REWARDS

The life of faith continually challenges us, but it rewards us too! The life of faith is not for the queasy or the reluctant. It is for those who aim toward full manhood and womanhood. For me, life becomes more and more exciting when I realize that *what I believe I will achieve.*

Dr. Karl Menninger, the eminent psychiatrist and founder of the Menninger Clinic in Topeka, Kansas, states that, "Attitudes are more important than facts." The doctor has seen attitudes, mind-sets, beliefs, and faith move mountains in people's lives.

Why? Because certain things in life are more important than facts. I've discovered it's not what we see in the mirror that matters; it is what we have in our hearts that makes the difference.

Each of us can go for the max and live life to the fullest, but in order to do so, we've gotta believe.

5

TURN
YOUR SCARS
INTO STARS

"When one door to happiness closes, another door always opens, but we often stand and look so long and so regretfully at the door that closes we fail to see the door that opens."

—Helen Keller

D r. Robert Schuller has become one of my best friends. We became close when his daughter, Carol, became a single-leg amputee due to an accident. I sent Dr. Schuller a copy of my book, *Strong at the Broken Places*, about my own personal recovery as an amputee. He invited me to join him one Sunday morning at church services in his marvelous Crystal Cathedral in Garden Grove, California. It was for me a fantastic experience to be on his popular TV program, "The Hour of Power." During the Christmas season of 1998, I returned to the Crystal Cathedral for one of the honors of my life. Dr. Schuller presented me with one of his "Scars into Stars" awards. He said that I had turned the "scars" of my life into my "stars." I was certainly glad he thought I had done that. I took it as a marvelous compliment! But that is what we all have to do in life if we are to go for the max—turn our scars into stars.

Elbert Hubbard, the marvelous American writer and philosopher at the turn of the century, once wrote that when we die and go to heaven, the Lord will not ask to see our medals. He will ask to see our scars! That's powerful.

We should look closely at our scars. They carry within them the stars of our future. We should examine our hurts, fears, and tragedies, but we should ultimately let them go. Otherwise, we will miss the opportunities that are ours. We should think about the closed doors in our lives and learn from them, but we should ultimately turn them over to God and focus our minds on the open doors of our lives.

When I was in the midst of my rehabilitation, struggling to blaze a new trail for myself, I stayed focused for a long time on the closed doors of my life. I was filled with regret. I was obsessed with missing limbs, lost opportunities, lost hopes. I couldn't see much good in the future. I had no idea whether I would live to see any of my dreams come true.

Before Vietnam, I had planned to enter politics in Georgia. That seed had been planted during my student days, when I spent a semester in the nation's capitol. I loved Washington. It was challenging. It was exciting. I dreamed that maybe one day I might run for public office and eventually rise to the Congress of the United States.

Later, while recuperating at Walter Reed Hospital in 1968, for a time I still fantasized about those early hopes. I dreamed of learning to walk on artificial limbs (without too noticeable a limp) and shaking hands with my good left hand (maybe others wouldn't notice my missing hand). By the time I was transferred to the Veterans Administration Hospital in Washington in 1969, however, those dreams seemed dashed. Such hopes seemed impossible. I was a wounded veteran of an unpopular war.

At that time I could not have imagined that the very *scars* of military service would later become the *stars* for my political victory. After returning to my hometown and receiving an enthusiastic welcome, press attention turned me into something of a local celebrity. The media portrayed me as a war hero, though I certainly didn't feel like one. I could relate to President Kennedy on this. When someone asked the former young naval officer how he became a war hero, Kennedy responded: "Simple. They sank my boat."

Simple for me too. The grenade went off!

My *scars* turned me into a "celebrity." Those *scars* helped open the doors for me in politics. Valuable name recognition came from the celebrity status, and when I ran for the Georgia State Senate in 1970, it helped me win my first political race. My scars had become my stars!

CANCEL ALL EXCUSES

Shakespeare once wrote, "There's a divinity which shapes our ends, rough-hew them how we will." My ends had become pretty rough-hewn. However, I was beginning to see some shaping of them by a divine hand.

Some doors in life had closed, but others were opening.

In those days, I began learning that despite our rough-hewn lives, nothing need stop us from becoming the person God wants us to be. My enthusiasm picked up. My morale improved. I now had a daily challenge to become a good state senator. I was beginning to get back on track with my life!

Since those early struggles in my own life and political career, I have learned that having one's life "rough-hewn" is just God's way of shaping us. No matter what doors shut, others seem to open. And no matter how low life sinks, there's always hope. As Henry Wadsworth Longfellow phrased it, "The lowest ebb is the turn of the tide."

People who refuse to fixate on closed doors always inspire me. I love the story of a man named David Ring. He lives in Orlando, Florida. David was born with cerebral palsy. He recalls that kids in his school made fun of his awkward gait and the involuntary facial contortions which happened when he tried to communicate.

As he approached his twenties, David says he was a mama's boy, insecure, someone with only a meager education. His hopes for the future seemed dim. A job, a marriage, and a family seemed impossible.

Still, David could not forget the faith his mother always held in him during her lifetime—her encouragement, the pain she felt when he stumbled, the joy she expressed when he succeeded. David Ring knew his mother never gave up on him, and this helped him not to give up on himself.

One day David determined to get a life of his own. He vowed he would become the person God intended him to be . . . a capable adult with a job and a family. He decided to go for the max! Today, in his thirties, he serves as an ordained evangelist with an international Christian ministry. He speaks to congregations worldwide. He motivates audiences on every continent. His theme: "Shine, Don't Whine."

"I've got cerebral palsy, " he announces. "What's your excuse?"

David Ring deeply believes there's no excuse for not blooming where we are planted. It's hard to imagine there can be any valid excuse for *not* rising and shining where we are today. His example made me see it's time for *me* to shine, not whine too!

> *Arise, shine; for thy light is come, and the glory of the LORD is risen upon thee.*
>
> —Isaiah 60:1

One of my U.S. Senate colleagues is Ted Kennedy. He lives with his lovely wife, Vicki, in their home on the famous Kennedy compound in Hyannisport, Massachusetts. The house contains many photos of the large Kennedy clan, several of whom have died tragically. On a piano in the living room, there's a small brass plaque which reads: "The world cares not about the storms you encounter, but only whether you bring home the ship."

I have had the honor of meeting and working with many Kennedy family members for a generation and have observed this about each one: They don't whine. They shine. They turn their scars into stars.

God has worked things out in my life so that my scars have become stars. He has put good people in my life who have helped me do that too! One day in 1969, a V.A. hospital staff member,

Eddie Griggs, said something to me that flipped on a switch in my mind. Eddie was a survivor of the Normandy beachhead landing on June 6, 1944. He had lost most of his unit that day. He himself had been blown up, losing a leg to a land mine.

"I try to put the past behind me," Eddie said. "I have this little boat, and I love to get in that boat, go out on the water, fish, and just be by myself. It's my *'thing.'*"

I wasn't big on boats, but I was big on politics. As time passed, Eddie's philosophy took root in me. Analyze the past, the failure, the disaster—whatever blew up in your face—then put it squarely behind you.

I owe a lot to Eddie and his words of wisdom. He is deceased now, but his advice is still solid. When we analyze whatever it was that happened, then focus not on what we lost, but on what remains, we move into new clarity of purpose. Eddie's words helped return me to my own life's purpose. Eddie encouraged me to turn my scars into stars and to continue to live life to the fullest.

MOVING PAST THE FIELD OF LOSSES

People who are able to put scars behind them and turn them into stars impress me. I love the story of the young man who sold papers for the *Kansas City Star* on the edge of town. Often he'd huddle on windy street corners, pulling the newspaper close to him for shelter. In those days, he vowed he'd never again be cold. He promised himself he'd do whatever it took to stay warm.

"Our deepest fear is not that we are inadequate, our deepest fear is that we are powerful beyond measure. It is our light, not our darkness that most frightens us. We ask ourselves, who am I to be brilliant, gorgeous, talented, and fabulous? Actually, who are you not to be? You are a child of God. Your playing small doesn't serve the world. There is nothing enlightened about shrinking, so that other people won't feel insecure around you. You were born to make manifest the glory of God within us. It is not just in some of us; it is in everyone. And, as we let our own light shine, we unconsciously give other people permission to do the same. As we are liberated from our own fear, our presence automatically liberates others."

—Nelson Mandela

As a daily newspaper reader, he noticed the cartoons. He soon began drawing his own. His first, "Oswald the Rabbit," was classified as a failure. During those early days of struggle, the young man experienced personal bankruptcy, then deep emotional depression.

This cartoonist continued to draw. His name? Walt Disney. He later turned his scars into stars—stars like Mickey Mouse and Donald Duck. Walt Disney would never again be cold!

Disney summed it up this way: "All our dreams can come true if we but have the courage to pursue them."

I also love the story of Thomas Edison, the great American inventor. Edison's grade school teachers said he was too stupid to learn. In fact, Edison had a relatively common malady which would be diagnosed today as dyslexia—not a learning disability, but a reading disability. Edison was denied formal schooling. His school-teacher mother tutored the boy and encouraged him to follow his interests. Soon he became fascinated by the world of science. He began to explore it, tinkering in his basement with chemicals and projects of all kinds.

Edison claimed his first patent—for the ticker tape machine—at age nineteen! Many other breakthrough inventions followed. When he was introduced to an audience as the inventor of the "talking machine," the astonishing phonograph, Edison quipped that God invented the talking machine, he had just invented one you could turn off!

At the Thomas Edison Laboratory opposite Edison's winter home in Fort Myers, Florida, you can see a poignant reminder of an incredible man who turned his scars into stars. The wooden casing surrounding Edison's phonograph has some curious marks . . . teeth marks made by Edison. The great inventor, deafened by a boyhood injury, "listened" to music by clamping his teeth on the phonograph case. The music's vibrations reached his jaw muscles, activating tendons in the inner ear near the audio nerve. Thus, Edison "heard" music. He had turned the scars of increasing deafness into the stars of inventions like the phonograph which, ironically, could bring music into the lives of millions.

One of the hallmarks of Edison's success was that he turned his failures into success. He tried thousands of experiments before he finally perfected the light bulb. Edison, though, quipped that he had not failed thousands of times; he just knew thousands of things that didn't work! Edison once accidentally knocked over a glass of milk on his desk. He turned that accident into his invention of waxed paper! Edison never seemed to look back at closed doors. He continued to walk through the doors that opened. Because Thomas Edison continued to turn his scars into stars, he became the most prolific inventor of the twentieth century.

Other brilliant, distinguished Americans also have been dyslexic, yet they succeeded by turning their scars into stars. As a youngster, the dyslexic Albert Einstein was labeled "not too bright." He went on to develop the basic theory behind the atom bomb. General George S. Patton, Jr., another dyslexic, was accepted into West Point but almost failed academically. He said, however, that his reading difficulties made him only "try harder." That work paid off immeasurably when his country called him to lead American troops against the toughest defenses of the Third Reich during World War II. Patton prevailed. He helped change world history.

Helen Keller suffered a fever at age eighteen months which left her blind, deaf, and mute. Tutored as a young girl by Ann Sullivan, her "miracle worker" friend, she went on to become a college graduate, author, founder of the Books for the Blind program of the Library of Congress, challenger of the Lions Club International to help the sight-impaired, and a world-acclaimed humanitarian.

Admiral Richard E. Byrd became the first person to fly over the North Pole and the South Pole—after being retired from the United States Navy as too disabled for service.

Another young man, twenty-one years old, tried to learn the retail sales business. But his boss in the store where he worked as a clerk had little confidence in him. He actually denied the youthful clerk opportunities for sales, claiming he didn't have enough sense to "meet the public." The young man turned his scars into stars. He went on to found the greatest retail chain of his day. His name was F. W. Woolworth.

Julius Caesar, Napoleon Bonaparte, and Alexander the Great all had epilepsy. But each man turned his scars into a brilliant, star-studded career.

A century ago, a young American woman thought she had a talent for writing. After submitting several stories to a publisher, she was advised to give up writing and go back to her sewing. However, young Louisa May Alcott continued to believe in herself. She would often write until her fingers bled. Eventually, in a day when few women attempted to write for publication, Louisa produced a book which became an American classic—*Little Women*. Other books followed, and the woman who had endured the privations of her nation's Civil War and a dismaying lack of professional encouragement, became solidly established among America's most beloved authors. She turned her scars into stars.

> *"Never consent to creep when you feel the impulse to soar."*
> —*Helen Keller*

By the late 1930s, Winston Churchill had been counted out politically. During World War I his career had been hampered by a British naval disaster for which he took full responsibility. By late 1940, however, England had become the focus of an all-out attack from Hitler's army and air corps. Following the failure of Prime Minister Neville Chamberlain's policy of appeasement and his subsequent resignation, the king of England called Churchill to Buckingham Palace to form a new government.

> *"Seeing much, suffering much, and studying much are the three pillars of learning."*
>
> —*Benjamin Disraeli*

Offered both the office of prime minister and that of minister of defense, Churchill accepted. As he left the royal palace, Churchill later recalled, "It seemed as if all my life had been but a preparation for that moment." From the ashes of perceived ignominy and the scars of disgrace, Churchill rose to become a star in the history of modern civilization!

SHINING UP OUR DREAMS

Our responsibility is to prepare. Our responsibility is to believe. Our responsibility is to muster the courage to move forward in faith by the grace of God and with the help of friends. It is our Father's place to know the time and the season of our blossoming and success.

Ours must be the daily ritual of watching for our moment to come. We must be ready when the spotlight focuses on us . . . and our moment will come.

What of missed opportunities? What of past disasters? What of past failures? These are in the past; leave them there. They are the closed doors. Look to the open ones. The real challenge of life is to live in the now and to plan for the future. We must look forward and look up. Our job is to stop whining and start shining.

As Churchill told his comrades in the midst of World War II, "Lift up your hearts. All will come right."

Dr. Benjamin Mays, son of a former slave, was a native Georgian. Dr. Mays overcame abject poverty and devastating lack of opportunity to become chairman of the board of education for Atlanta, Georgia, as well as president of the prestigious Morehouse College in that city. He turned his scars into stars. He continually challenged his students with these words:

> It must be borne in mind that the tragedy in life doesn't lie in not reaching your goal. The tragedy lies in having no goal to reach. It isn't a calamity to die with dreams unfulfilled, but it is a calamity not to dream. It isn't a disaster to be unable to capture your ideal, but it is a disaster to have no ideal to capture. It isn't a disgrace not to reach for the stars, but it is a disgrace to have no stars to reach for. Not failure, but low aim is the sin.[2]

Ours is not to cry over spilt milk. Ours is to milk the most from every day and aim high in the future. Ours is to focus not on our scars but on our stars. As Dr. Robert Schuller also says, "Set your goals by your hopes—rather than your hurts."

We can go for the max in our lives if we are determined to turn our scars into scars!

6 THINK POSITIVELY

"Positive thinking is realistic thinking. It always sees the negative, but it doesn't dwell on the negative and nurture it, letting it dominate the mind. It keeps the negative in proper size, and grows the positive big. Thus, it enables countless men and women to have serenity and power— despite continuing pain."

—Dr. Norman Vincent Peale

During the 1950s, Dr. Norman Vincent Peale, senior minister at Marble Collegiate Church in New York City, wrote *The Power of Positive Thinking*. It became one of the best-sellers of all time. At first, however, the book's premise struck many other clerics and critics as far too simplistic for their sophisticated times. Many laughed it to scorn. Dr. Peale, however, accepted the widespread jeers and condescending remarks with humility and a positive outlook—until time proved him right.

More than four decades later, science has learned much about the human brain, the mind, and the value of programming one's thinking with positives. Today nobody argues with the idea that positive thinking produces positive results. More than half a century has passed since William James stated, "The greatest discovery of my generation is that a human being can alter his life by altering his attitude." Ancient writing confirms this thought. King Solomon once observed, "For as [a man] thinketh in his heart, so *is* he" (Prov. 23:7).

My parents endowed me with many good things, but perhaps one of the most important was their examples of strong, positive thinking. For this reason, I found it natural to *expect* to achieve during my growing-up years. Lucky is the boy or girl who has such parents.

REALISM OR NEGATIVITY?

Lucy, the *Peanuts* cartoon character, was once shown sitting with her head in her hands, looking depressed. The matter-of-fact miss was saying in one comic strip, "I only dread one day at a time." Our Creator does not intend us to dread one day at a time. We are meant, I believe, to *live* one day at a time. As a matter of fact, I believe we are meant to live life to the fullest and go for the max every day!

Most of us are so geared to the negatives of life that we agree with George Carlin, the comedian, who jokes that "Positive thinking is miscalculation." We come to believe that surely the world was not organized for good. We convince ourselves that certainly it was not organized for *our* good! Those who believe the world has capitulated to evil naturally believe it would be "miscalculation" to anticipate good for *themselves*.

Realistically, however, this attitude ignores one fact. The Book of Genesis records that after God created the world, He called it "very good." Since God calls our world "very good," why shouldn't we?

Positive thinking is *not* miscalculation. I've found it to be the way life works best.

Positive thinking is more important to us than we know. Dr. Peale once pointed out that it takes ten positives to overcome one negative. We need as many positives in our lives as we can get! When we begin to look beyond our personal scars and focus on our stars, we find we are starting to think and act positively. I've discovered that when I can be positive, even toward negative situations, positive results occur. Positive results, of course, move us forward. Positive thinking about our goals, our dreams, our aspirations helps us to go for the max and live a more fulfilling life.

Call this philosophy anything you choose. Call it *positive thinking*, with Dr. Norman Vincent Peale; *possibility thinking*, with Dr. Robert Schuller; or *positive mental attitude*, with W. Clement Stone, the well-known Chicago insurance executive. Whatever term we choose, it means thinking, acting, and reacting *affirmatively*. It means thinking positively in love and faith, not negatively in fear and distrust of other people, circumstances, happenings, and life events.

Easy to say, but I've found I really have to work at it! Why? Negativity is all around. I find I must *focus* my thoughts toward healthy, positive ends. It's easy to talk the talk, hard to walk the walk.

That's okay. I've discovered God loves me anyhow. I've found that when I fail to respond positively to negative situations. I'm human. I have to lighten up. I've found I must not judge myself or someone else too harshly.

Meanwhile, I try to practice a positive approach to my challenges. I've found positive thinking really works!

EFFECTIVE THINKING IN ACTION

My first mentor in politics was a man of great positive thinking. James A. Mackay became a congressman from Georgia in the mid 1960s. Volunteering in his campaign, in

> *"Sin is when one thinks they are more than they are, or less than they are, or anything other than who they are."*
>
> —*Tom Malone*

1964, was my first political experience. In 1965 I worked as an intern in his Washington, D.C. office.

He was and is one of the most positive people I have ever met. He told me about his mother, who lived to be almost one hundred years old and once was a missionary to China.

Mr. Mackay pointed out to me that the strongest Bible verse which influenced his mother was in Paul's letter to the Philippians (Phil. 4:8) in which Paul admonishes the church at Phillipi to think only good things:

> Whatsoever things are true, whatsoever things are honest, whatsoever things are just, whatsoever things are pure, whatsoever things are lovely, whatsoever things are of good report; if there be any virtue, and if there be any praise, think on these things.

I've found this verse very helpful in keeping my mind focused on the better things in life.

Dr. Dennis Kimbro, author of *Think and Grow Rich: A Black Choice*, also believes in the power of positive thinking. He writes:

> Ignorance is no longer an adequate excuse for failure. Why? Because virtually all limitation is self-imposed. You

will soon realize that you, the individual, are a minute expression of the Creator of all things and as such, you have no limitations except those accepted in your own mind. Every man and woman has within himself or herself a sleeping giant. No one needs to be less than he or she is. There rests within each of us the power to become great—each in our own way.[3]

■ ■ ■

A personal hero of mine was a powerful, never-say-die positive thinker. As a young Navy lieutenant, he and his men became shipwrecked in the Solomon Islands during World War II. The party had to survive on their own. The sailors soon became discouraged. They didn't know where they were. The U.S. Navy didn't know where they were. Their boat had been sunk. The Japanese were just one island away.

As morale dropped, the men began to mutter among themselves about the difficulties they were enduring. Perhaps it would be better to surrender, their conversation went. As

> *"Everything can be taken from a man except the last of human freedoms—to choose one's attitudes in any given set of circumstances."*
> —*Viktor E. Frankl*

prisoners of war, at least they might receive medical treatment, and they would be identified. Surely this would be better than dying without a trace on a deserted island. Pessimism was rampant. The men were almost ready to give up.

The lieutenant stepped into the crowd of men and addressed their concerns. "We're gonna get out of here, believe me!" he encouraged. *"We're gonna make it!"*

Something about his demeanor made his shipmates believe him. Their hope was renewed. One seaman pulled the lieutenant aside and demanded to know why he could be so positive. "I guess it's a character defect," the lieutenant wisecracked.

That character defect eventually led the Navy officer and his small band of men to safety. Later, the lieutenant received a medal for saving their lives. His character defect was to lead him to the United States House of Representatives, the United States Senate, and finally to the presidency of the United States of America.

His name was John F. Kennedy.

Johnny Mercer, the famed Academy Award-winning songwriter, enjoyed a Broadway and Hollywood career which spanned four decades. Among his more than two hundred songs, Mercer published a cute little ditty which became a runaway hit during America's darkest days of World War II. Mercer's gift to our war-weary but gallant nation featured irresistible lyrics set to a bouncy swing tune, "Accent-uate the Positive."

Members of that generation heard those words sung on the battlefront, at U.S.O. dances, along wartime assembly lines . . . everywhere. "Ac-cen-tuate the positive" seemed to become in those days a watchword for America's thinking.

■ ■ ■

When I was a young lieutenant and before I went to the war of my generation, I used to visit the church of Dr. Peale. I was stationed at Ft. Monmouth, New Jersey, in 1966. I enjoyed spending weekends in New York where I saw the sights, dated, and partied on Saturdays. But I often found my way to Marble Collegiate Church on Sundays.

Sometimes I had stayed out so late on Saturday that I dozed in church the next day, but I always paid full attention to Dr. Peale's words. His messages, simple and affirmative, hit home. They made you think. You remembered his thoughts through-out the next week. His words reinforced my basic instincts to think positively about life and living. His sermons encouraged me to go for the max and live life to the fullest in every way.

Dr. Peale and his wife, Ruth, influenced my life for more than three decades. From those Sundays during the 1960s when I would enter the tall, imposing Fifth Avenue church and join throngs of lively worshipers inside . . . enjoy the service and especially the sermon . . . grab an after-church sandwich in the fellowship hall . . . choose several pamphlets in the narthex . . .

then head back to my Army post in New Jersey . . . my mind and thinking received tremendous nourishment, and my spirit thrived. The truths Dr. Peale preached electrified me.

> *"If you firmly imagine that you are a person destined for success, success is what you ultimately will have. If you are convinced that you will fail, failure will stalk you no matter where you go. If you think scarcity, it will befall you. If you imagine abundance flowing to you, it will flow."*
>
> —*Norman Vincent Peale*

When I served as administrator of the Veterans Administration during the Carter presidency, *GUIDEPOSTS*, the interfaith magazine founded by the Peales, interviewed me for an article. My friendship with the Peales deepened. During the 1980s, Dr. Peale and I shared the same speaking platform from time to time.

It was always fun to be in Dr. Peale's presence. He was the real thing, the genuine article. Small in stature, somewhat shy, Dr. Peale exhibited the heart of a lion when he spoke to audiences about a person's God-given potential to achieve great things.

As friendly and unassuming as he was, I nevertheless was always in awe of this wonderful man. Dr. Peale had become one of the most notable teachers, preachers, speakers, and authors of the twentieth century. He possessed a powerful ability to help his listeners think and move in more positive directions in their lives. But Peale himself had had his own problems with feelings of inferiority in growing up.

As a young boy, Norman Vincent Peale once approached his minister father, head down, obviously bothered, but reluctant to say what was on his mind. The father waited a bit, and at last the youngster confessed that he felt so terribly inferior that he even disliked his name. He wanted to change it.

> *"Our life becomes what our thoughts make of it."*
> —*Marcus Aurelius*

The father was stunned. How could he teach young Norman to take pride in his family's heritage? How could he teach him to wear the Peale name with honor? The child continued to insist. He wanted a new name.

The father lovingly began to counsel his son. He spoke to his feelings of unworthiness. He assured him that everyone experiences such feelings. When he needed help, he told young Norman, he should pray to God for strength.

Meanwhile, he could not change his name. The father looked at his son and said, with firm finality: "You will always be known as Norman Vincent Peale."

That day a loving father encouraged his son's thinking toward a positive path. The young boy grew into a man whose powerful mind-set reinforced countless people like me to focus on the good in life rather than the bad. This way of thinking has helped me survive some of the toughest times of my life.

■ ■ ■

Positive thinking for me means not losing sight of those things which Dr. Benjamin Mays said it would be a tragedy to live without: goals, dreams, ideals, and stars. It has helped me to remember to "ac-cent-uate the positive."

I've found in my life that if I think, believe, and act positively, rather than negatively, good things will come to me. These good things God wants us to have, I believe. I've discovered that if we focus daily on our dreams, ambitions, goals, and hopes, and expect positive results, in God's good time He will give us our heart's desires. It will be His good pleasure to give us the kingdom! We can go for the max in our lives if we think positively!

7
REACH FOR THE SKY

"We never know how high we are
Till we are called to rise;
And then, if we are true to plan,
Our statures touch the skies."

—Emily Dickinson

P resident Kennedy became the master of the televised presidential press conference in the early 1960s. Witty, thoughtful, engaging, and persuasive, his personal charisma and charm could win over even the most skeptical reporters. Once a newsman blurted out, "Mr. President, are you happy in your job?" President Kennedy's response was striking.

The President said the ancient Greeks defined happiness as the full exercise of all a person's powers along the lines of excellence. The President stated that according to **that** definition, he was happy.

Today there's a great obsession with the concept of excellence. Many books have been written on the subject. Major American corporations seek even more effective means by which American business can compete successfully in the global marketplace. Most of us understand that our prosperity, personal and national, depends on our reaching toward a more excellent way in all things pertaining to individual, community, and business life.

Personally, I've found excellence as a concept is like reaching for the sky. You may never get there, but you're better because you try. Actually, just reaching for the sky makes me happy. My worst disappointments in life have resulted from those times when I aimed too low. But I've always had the time of my life, even if I didn't hit the bull's eye, whenever I aimed high.

In the minds of the ancient Greeks, there was little mystery about excellence. Excellence meant more than happiness; it meant something you did every day. Aristotle, the classic Greek philosopher, observed that "Excellence is a habit."

When I was playing basketball in high school, there was an old adage about basketball practice. The coaches used to tell us, "What you do in practice is what you will do in a game." Each day is a real game for us all. We better practice like it too! If we are to achieve excellence, we must reach for it every day!

EXPECT THE BEST—ALWAYS

Bobby Knight, the University of Indiana basketball coach, offers a succinct definition for his players about what he expects of their discipline: "Do it right the first time and do it that way every time." That is a commitment to excellence. That's reaching for the sky.

The Greeks not only gave us their noble concept of excellence, but also they gave us a great way to showcase it—the Olympic Games. When I watch the Olympics, I am inspired. I can identify with the athletes as they run. I enter their skins as they jump and strain for that extra ounce of strength that will take them over the top. Each performance seems to mirror the inner struggle I face to be the best I can become.

The Olympic Games remind me that life should never be a humdrum exercise. Olympians demonstrate to me that we should all be reaching for the sky, no matter who we are or where we come from. The games remind me that there are goals to be achieved, obstacles to be overcome, excellence to be achieved in life. The games also tell us that we never have to live defeated lives. They send the exciting message that all of us can go for the max!

> *"First say to yourself what you would be:*
> *and then do what you have to do."*
> —*Ralph Waldo Emerson*

LIFTING PERCEIVED LIMITS

Many people, however, don't even try to do better or be better. Because they know they are not perfect, they don't put out the effort! But excellence in the classic Greek sense denotes the act of *trying* to be our best. Excellence is about *pursuit* as well as *achievement*. It's about the *journey*, not just the *destination*. Coach Vince Lombardi's famous motto reminds us: "Winning is not everything—but making effort to win is."

SHOOT PAST THE DISCOMFORT ZONE

In my own early struggles during a year and a half of reha-bilitation, I often wondered whether it would be physically possible to climb out of that valley, much less reach for the sky. Actually reaching for a glass of water seemed difficult enough.

The idea of walking on artificial limbs or driving a car seemed impossible.

During those terrible times, however, two amazing books inspired me to reach for the sky. One was *Psycho-Cybernetics*, a best-selling book written by the eminent plastic surgeon and author, Dr. Maxwell Maltz. His book offered me a fascinating approach to life. It encouraged me to continue to strive to improve. Dr. Maltz's book explained that our minds are programmed in much the same way that computers in the world of cybernetics are programmed. Dr. Maltz observed that whenever we program ourselves toward achieving challenging goals, we move *forward*. Our psychological state becomes one of focusing not on failure, but on achievement. However, when our goals become thwarted by pain, tragedy, hurt, disappointment, disfigurement, or other negative circumstances, our mental and emotional balance suffers. Dr. Maltz compared this to riding a bicycle. He pointed out that as long as we exert our efforts in a positive direction, we maintain our sense of happiness and well-being. We maintain our balance. However, if we become diverted from our goal and stop pedaling, we begin to waiver.

Dr. Maltz's book offered me encouragement to keep "pedaling," to keep believing in life, believing in my goals, believing that in truth, a better life was possible. It's encouraging to me to realize that just *continuing to reach for the sky* equates to excellence—and this is the pathway to victory and success.

A STORY OF EXCELLENCE

The second book which inspired me was an incredible story. The title? You guessed it! *Reach for the Sky.* It was written about the life of Doug Bader, a legless fighter pilot of World War II. Captain Jack Lawton, my old friend at Walter Reed Hospital, sent me the paperback version in hopes that it might encourage me. It did! "Nasty Jack," as I called him, left Walter Reed in 1968, volunteered for his third tour of duty in Vietnam, and while there discovered the slender volume and forwarded it to me.

Bader's story had a profound impact on me. Bader was a hotshot young pilot in the British Royal Air Force before World War II. Just prior to the war, he cracked up his plane. The accident cost him both legs. Eventually he was discharged from the R.A.F. as "totally disabled."

As Hitler's blitz hammered Great Britain, England needed every trained pilot they could find. By now Doug Bader had become proficient on artificial limbs. He clamored to return to active duty. Incredibly, he came back in the R.A.F. and was given flight status!

The story captivated me. I especially identified with Bader's difficulties in struggling to walk on his artificial limbs. Bader had retained one knee, so strategic to his rehabilitation. It gave him balance to walk and later provided him the ability to use aircraft pedals. Unfortunately, I had no knees and only one arm. Nevertheless, Bader's story inspired me to reach for the sky. If Doug Bader could retrain himself to become the great pilot he once had been, I believed I could do something worthwhile with my life.

Upon his return to active duty with the Royal Air Force, Bader put together a marvelous war record. He shot down twenty-six enemy planes and rose to the rank of wing commander.

Then Bader was shot down over enemy territory. He became a P.O.W. in Germany. He escaped, only to be recaptured! Finally, the Germans placed him in a maximum security prison to sit out the rest of the war.

The book tells the story of Bader's being shot down. His plane was hit by enemy ground fire. As it plunged to the ground in flames, Bader managed to leap from the aircraft, but he left one of his artificial legs behind. Once he was safe on the ground, the Germans easily captured him. They were so astonished and impressed at their prisoner's courage, however, that they allowed the R.A.F. to drop an artificial limb for their prisoner to use. When Bader strapped on the limb, the German officers raised their glasses in a toast of respect.

At war's end, the British celebrated the fifth anniversary of what Churchill called "The Battle of Britain." On September 15, 1945, Wing Commander Doug Bader was chosen to lead the fly-past over London in honor of the occasion. For his incredible courage in World War II, Bader received the Victoria Cross, England's highest military decoration.

Doug Bader's story still impacts me today. I am a better person for knowing about a man who refused to let anything stand between him and his reaching for the sky. In 1995 I had a very meaningful postscript to my involvement with the Bader story when, during a visit to London, the British government gave me an opportunity to tour the rehabilitation center where Bader had gone through his painful struggle to become stronger at *his* broken places. With emotion, I saw his artificial limbs and the training area where he had sweated for endless days and months to become the man he wanted to be. I realized vividly once again the daily toil that excellence requires. It was a silent reminder to me of how much effort, pain, and struggle reaching for the sky always involves. Afterwards, I witnessed the dedication of the new Doug Bader Sports Center in that same facility—a fitting memorial indeed!

In every way, Doug Bader exemplified the Royal Air Force motto: "Per Ardua Ad Astra"—"through adversity to the stars!" Later, while serving as head of the Veterans Administration during the 1970s, I wrote to Doug Bader and told him how he had inspired me. He replied with a beautiful letter that I will treasure for the rest of my life.

Doug Bader died a few years later, and I'm so glad I made contact with this wonderful human being before he passed away. He encouraged me to reach for the sky and enabled me to believe I could do it.

> *"To be what we are, and to become*
> *what we are capable of becoming,*
> *is the only end of life."*
> —*Robert Louis Stevenson*

When we commit ourselves to reach for the sky . . . live life as a daring adventure . . . keep the faith with ourselves and our goals and turn our scars into stars, something marvelous happens to us. We discover vibrant new energy and a rekindled zest for living. As we reach smaller goals along the way and achieve little conquests, we "program" joy and happiness into every day of our existence.

THE PRICE OF EXCELLENCE

Reaching for the sky, though, is very frustrating for me. But I've learned I never move from where I am to where I want to be unless I start to achieve a bigger and better goal than the one I have at the time.

One of my hardest lessons in reaching a goal was my attempt to learn the game of tennis. I was a slow learner. I couldn't hit the ball right. I had a weak backhand. My serve often drove the ball into the net. One of the most reassuring things I remember from those days, though, was someone's advice that "you never get better until you play against someone better than yourself."

That someone better was Edgar Abbott—my boyhood friend. He had placed second in the state in high school tennis singles four years in a row. The idea of reaching higher helped me persevere through the difficult early stages of learning how to play tennis against someone who constantly beat me.

Doug Bader maintained that the greatest personal satisfaction he experienced following his injury was in beating the golfer who had taught him how to play the game. I can well understand, since I remember feeling that same elation when I finally beat Edgar, the man who taught me to play, in my city's championship tennis game in 1960. I still to this day cherish the moment.

However, we don't experience the thrill of such accomplishments unless we reach for the sky. We don't enjoy meaningful achievements unless we are determined to go for the max. As St. Augustine wrote, "What you are must always displease, if you are to attain to that which you are not."

But what about failure along the way? We must expect it. Abraham Lincoln's wisdom holds much truth:

> One night in November, a shower of meteors fell from the clear night sky. A friend standing by was frightened. But I looked up and between the falling stars I saw the fixed stars beyond, shining serene in the firmament, and I said, 'Let us not mind the meteors, let us keep our eyes on the stars.'

The meteors of momentary failures may shower down from time to time, but I like Henry Ford's viewpoint: "Failure is only

> *"Lives of great men all remind us,*
> *We can make our lives sublime,*
> *And departing, leave behind us*
> *Footprints in the sands of time."*
> —*Henry Wadsworth Longfellow*

the opportunity to more intelligently begin again." Mary Pickford, the silent screen star, once observed, "Falling is not failing! You only fail when you don't try again."

Dr. Maltz offered a practical outlook on failure when he wrote: "Remember, you will not always win. Some days, the most resourceful individual will taste defeat. But, there is in this case, always tomorrow—after you have done your best to achieve success today."

Reach for the sky! If you have any desire to be great in tennis, go for it. If you have any notion of becoming outstanding in business, you must determine to take your best shot.

Whatever the personal goal you wish to achieve, you must commit to becoming bigger and better than you are today. You must understand and accept that it's often a painful process which enables us to ultimately beat those who taught us how to play. The process may be arduous, fatiguing, and endlessly discouraging—but it's *possible!*

PRESS
ON!

"Life is not easy for any of us. But what of that? We must have perseverance and above all, confidence in ourselves. We must believe that we are gifted for something, and that this thing, at whatever cost, must be attained."

—Madame Curie

A touch of winter nipped the air in Vietnam near our base camp in An Khe in late 1967. A brisk breeze blew our jungle fatigue uniforms as we stood at attention in company formation. Normally, we would not be huddled together as a unit! We would be at our outposts scattered throughout the Central Highlands of Vietnam with the First Air Cavalry Division. This, however, was a special day. We were in formation to salute the raising of our new company flag.

In the military, a flag symbolizes the heart and soul of the unit. Our first sergeant, "Top" Marcus, had made the first flag for our company, and we were determined to raise it there in Vietnam right where our small signal unit was based. Earlier, Captain Mike Barry, our company commander, had given instructions to Sergeant Marcus to go into the nearby village and negotiate with the local Vietnamese for the cloth we would need. Sergeant Marcus had a good deal of experience with the native peoples of Southeast Asia. During World War II he had served as a young signalman with Merrill's Marauders in Burma. We weren't surprised when he returned with some fine cloth bought at a good price.

Soon some of the company's young soldiers were put to sewing—and we had a flag! Sergeant Marcus proudly hooked it up to a tree (shaved of its bark) which we used as a flagpole. The sacred ceremony began. The flag was slowly raised and could be seen all over the division area. It was emblazoned

> *"Always bear in mind that your own resolution to succeed is more important than any one thing."*
>
> —*Abraham Lincoln*

with the famous oversized First Air Cavalry Division's horse head insignia with our company designation, "Company A, 13th Signal Battalion," beneath. Below that, our company motto stood out proudly as articulated by Captain Barry: "Press On!"

PRESS ON

The men stood at rapt attention. The bugler played. The cloth rose, unfurling slowly in the wind. As the flag touched the top of the pole, the men cheered. Our flag made a strong visual assertion that we in our little unit were committed to *press on* and survive this war.

Months later, I was wounded. One day, while lying in my hospital bed at Walter Reed Army Hospital, far from Vietnam and my unit, depressed and wondering what my future would hold and what I would do with my life, a package arrived from Vietnam. My old signal unit had sent the company flag to me!

As the ward nurses helped me unfold that unique, hand-sewn banner, the words *Press On* jumped out at me. Tears came to my eyes. I knew this was a powerful message to me from the men of my company. They were sending me a strong signal to press on with my life. In that immeasurably special way, they urged me not to give up. As I touched that cloth, my discouragement changed to resolve. Somehow I would press on . . . and get stronger even at the most broken places in my life.

I had my prized flag placed over my hospital bed so I could see it every day. I loved that old piece of cloth and its symbols. The flag represented not only the

> *"Any object will yield to persistence."*
> —*Leonardo da Vinci*

pride and honor of our unit, but also a dramatic and generous gesture of loyalty and support for me, from men with whom I had shared combat and seen so much of life and death. It also represented a never-say-die attitude: "Press on!"

In 1994, while serving as Georgia's Secretary of State, I wanted to show the men in our signal unit how much that flag meant to me. I was by law the custodian of Georgia's historic battle flags. I invited "Top" Marcus and other members of my old outfit to the Georgia State Capitol for a special ceremony. It was a small but happy collection of aging veterans. We hung the flag of Company A, 13th Signal Battalion, First Air Cavalry Division, on permanent display on the side of one of the walls of the capitol to stand proudly along with other battle flags from other wars.

There it remains today, as one of the more interesting artifacts in the long history of Georgia. Incidentally, the "First

Cav," as we called our division, had been formed in the early 1960s at Fort Benning in Columbus, Georgia, and had been sent from there to Vietnam by President Lyndon B. Johnson. In many ways it was Georgia's division in Vietnam.

The "Press On" motto is special to me. Wherever I am and whatever I am doing, I remember my buddies who shared with me the unique experiences of the Vietnam War. When we exchange Christmas cards, beside our signatures we write "Press On"—our special encouragement to one another. It's our special greeting which means, "Hang in there, keep the faith, we're still alive!"

Just two years after the flag dedication, I received the sad news that "Top" Marcus had died. Earlier, upon hearing he was ill, I had sent him a teddy bear with the words "Press On" emblazoned across the bear's chest. Top's brother told me it was the last thing he saw before he died.

As the years pass, in my own life, the "Press On" motto increases in meaning and importance to me. I often recall my days and nights as a young signal officer in combat in Vietnam. I remember times when it seemed impossible that I would survive. Still, by the grace of God and the help of many friends, medics, nurses, and therapists, I *did* survive. I feel deep gratitude to each of those who, with my endlessly encouraging parents, daily inspired this young soldier to *"Press On!"*

Sometimes in life, regardless of how well or ill we have lived it, life comes down to the simple question of whether or not we really want to survive. If the answer is yes, then sometimes all we can do is "press on."

Earl Nightingale, a marvelous radio commentator in the 1960s, once observed:

> When a child is born, he or she comes equipped with certain basic drives that psychologists have been listing for us for many years. And to my mind, one of the most interesting of these basic drives is the one we might call the drive to go on—the virtually indestructible tendency on the part of the human being to keep going, to wait for one more sunrise, to try just one more time, and then once more again, and again.[4]

■　■　■

In another era, another young cavalry officer learned the priceless value of pressing on. Winston Churchill served with the British forces during the Boer War. In fact, he engaged in the last cavalry charge on horseback in modern warfare. From that battle, he formed the witty notion: "There is nothing in life so exhilarating as being shot at without result!"

Later in the century, in the midst of World War II, when his countrymen were undergoing heavy Nazi bombing in London, the old cavalry officer returned to his alma mater, the Harrow School for Boys, to give a speech of encouragement to the young men. After a few preliminary words, Churchill simply stopped and surveyed the young faces in his audiences. He gazed intently into their eyes. What could he possibly say to young people in a country which was enduring such peril?

Then Churchill's voice rose. "Never give in. Never give in," he said. "Never. Never. Never!"

And that was it. The aging political and military genius took his seat. Applause thundered around him. That speech quickly became part of the Churchill legend. I never tire of hearing those words. What a powerful lesson expressed in so short a time!

DEVELOP SINGLE-MINDEDNESS

In terms of persistence, I love the story of a former football coach in south Georgia named Art Williams. Art began his career in the small town of Cairo, Georgia, where he had been hired to coach the local high school football team. When he took the job, the school was last in its region. A year later, the team reached the state finals.

One secret to Art's success was that he loved to motivate people. He was good at it. Like most coaches, though, he existed on a meager teacher's salary which was supplemented by his coach's pay. In those days he earned hardly enough to feed his family.

Art began to sell insurance on the side. But the part-time job did not appeal to him. He persisted, however, and eventually met a man who had a unique new perspective on the insurance business. At that time most insurance companies sold individuals policies which people would pay on all their lives, receiving small yearly dividends, and watching policy values increase slowly.

Williams's friend had a better idea—to sell term life insurance at a much lower price, allowing the consumer to invest the savings! The idea caught fire within Art Williams. He gave up coaching to risk building his new A. L. Williams Insurance Company.

His working capital? Hardly more than the phrase he coined: "Buy term and invest the rest." The company's early days were a struggle, but Williams had a vision and the determination to keep going until he succeeded.

He coached his fledgling sales team with the same fire which once led Cairo's high school team to success. He believed in his sales people. He often stated that every player on his team was a star. He liked to give rewards for good performance—T-shirts. In the early days it was the only gift he could afford.

With continuous effort and his unwavering determination to press on, Art Williams built a company which competed with the strongest insurance giants in America. When I spoke one year to the national convention of the A. L. Williams sales force at the Superdome in New Orleans, it was the largest audience I had ever addressed—forty thousand people. The fruits of one man's dogged persistence was impressive. Art Williams had built a large, highly motivated work force in America's insurance industry.

> *"Press on. Nothing in the world can take the place of persistence. Talent will not; nothing is more common than unsuccessful men with talent. Genius will not; unrewarded genius is almost a proverb. Education alone will not; the world is full of educated derelicts. Persistence and determination alone are omnipotent."*
>
> —*Attributed to Calvin Coolidge*

I knew that such impressive success had not come easily. But for Art Williams, pressing on had become the key to his astounding achievements. He would tell his rookie sales people, "For the first three years in your business, everything is going to go badly. Hang in there, though, and things will turn your way."

Williams ultimately sold his company for more than one billion dollars. Not bad for a high school coach from a small town who decided to leave the ruts . . . keep the faith . . . reach for the sky . . . think positively . . . and press on!

Many other American entrepreneurs have pressed on, persisted and become rich. For Art Williams, however, the real satisfaction was his knowledge that *he* not only gained financial security for his family, but that he also helped countless thousands of families understand how to gain financial security for *themselves*.

Not only did Art Williams press on to incredible success, but also he motivated thousands of other people to do the same!

DETERMINE TO PREVAIL

When I entered Georgia politics in the early 1970s, I met another young man who possessed outstanding qualities of dogged persistence. His family was not well-to-do. He had always worked hard for everything he had. This quiet, dedicated man had one important asset, however—a mother and father who had inspired him to set his goals and *press on toward* them.

With little money and barely any chance for a college education during World War II, the young man applied for admission to the U.S. Naval Academy. He was rejected. Unfortunately, he had flat feet.

Undaunted, he returned home and tried to correct the problem. He would roll his feet back and forth across a Coca-Cola bottle sometimes for hours in an effort to force his arches into correct position. Later, that young man was admitted to the Naval Academy. His name was Jimmy Carter.

At the time I first met Jimmy Carter, he was running for governor of Georgia. I was running for the state senate. The year was 1970. It was a hot July evening. Sweat was pouring off all of us. Carter had on a white short-sleeved shirt. His famous grin came through immediately. He was low-key, but "wound tight," as we in Georgia would say. He was fully committed to pressing on to win! Georgia Secretary of State, Ben Fortson, later described Jimmy Carter as being like a South Georgia turtle with his head up against a cypress stump. "You think that turtle can't move that stump," said Fortson, "but he just keeps pushing and pushing and pretty soon that stump is moved." Carter won the governorship and I won my state senate race. We've been lifelong friends ever since.

Carter had run for governor in 1966. He failed. But in the famous words of Babe Ruth, "It's hard to beat a person who won't give up." Jimmy Carter never gave up trying to be all he could be. He still hasn't!

The world would learn later of Carter's persistence in the face of adversity as he won the presidency in 1976 against overwhelming odds. Additionally, he surmounted incredible odds to put together the Middle East peace accords which still stand today. In 1981, he negotiated the release of Americans held hostage in Iran. He built the Carter Center in Atlanta. He has negotiated dozens of political issues in nations around the globe and is the best-known volunteer for Habitat for Humanity. One of the great strengths Jimmy Carter possesses is his ability to press on. He is another of my personal heroes.

Churchill often told the young politicians of his time not to worry about their slow advances in political life. He observed, "Only one link in the chain of destiny can be handled at a time!"

Sometimes the best thing and the *only* thing we can do is just "press on." The following poem by an unknown author expresses the thought:

When things go wrong as they sometimes will,

When the road you're trudging seems all uphill,

When the funds are low and the debts are high

And you want to smile but you have to sigh,

When care is pressing you down a bit,

Rest if you must, but don't you quit.

Success is failure turned inside out,

The silver tint of the clouds of doubt;

And you can never tell how close you are,

It may be near when it seems afar.

So, stick to the fight when you're hurt and hit—

It's when things go wrong that you mustn't quit.

WITH GOD THERE IS ALWAYS A WAY

An Olympic runner was asked the secret of his success. "The only way to win a race is to forget all previous victories which would give you false pride and all former failures which would give you false fears," he replied. "Each race is a new beginning. Pressing on to the finish tape is all that is important!"

The apostle Paul expressed that same thought in his letter to the Philippians (3:13–14) in which he wrote, "Brethren, I count not myself to have apprehended: but this one thing I do, forgetting those things which are behind, and reaching forth unto those things which are before, I press toward the mark for the prize of the high calling of God in Christ Jesus."

> *"I do not think there is any other quality so essential to success of any kind as the quality of perseverance."*
>
> —*John D. Rockefeller*

I like another line by Paul: "We are pressed on every side by troubles, but we are not crushed and broken. We are perplexed, but we don't give up and quit. We are hunted down, but God never abandons us. We get knocked down, but we get up again and keep going" (2 Cor. 4:8–9, NLT).

THE MAGNIFICENT REWARDS OF PERSISTENCE

The truth is that nothing significant can be achieved without grit, determination, and perseverance. Of all the lessons my life has taught me, I remain convinced that regardless of what happens to us, if we want to go for the max in life and achieve our full potential, we must "press on."

9

LET GOD WORK OUT THINGS

And we know that God causes everything to work together for the good of those who love God and are called according to his purpose for them.

—*Romans 8:28, NLT*

All too often, and especially when I sense failure gripping me by the throat, I don't feel "religious." In fact, that's the last thing I feel. But, if we have any faith at all, we know that it's at times like these when we should reach out to our Creator. I've learned the wisdom of doing that.

At times I have prayed only because the tide of problems was about to sink me. However, the older I get the more I realize the value of a daily spiritual connection with God.

The need for this daily walk is something I've learned while moving through many crises in my life. I've found I do need the Lord—for guidance, strength, endurance. I've learned the necessity of "letting go and letting God." As Dr. Lloyd Ogilvie, the marvelous U.S. Senate Chaplain puts it, "Things don't work out. God works out things." My spiritual discipline now is to let God work out things in my life.

LEARNING GOD-RELIANCE

While serving as head of the V. A. during the late 1970s, I once visited the Grand Ole Opry in Nashville, Tennessee, as the guest of a local congressman. We were to present an award to the show for a Christmas album they had produced. The album, hosted by Johnny Cash, featured many famous country music performers. It was done for veterans at V.A. hospitals around the nation.

I had never visited the Grand Ole Opry before, but I had certainly enjoyed listening to it on my little AM radio while growing up in Georgia. The 50,000-watt clear-channel signal on radio station WSM out of Nashville was strong enough to reach all across the South. The Grand Ole Opry and its performers were legendary to me.

As I was listening to the radio show in my hometown in Georgia, I didn't know it, but I was going to grade school with a future Grand Ole Opry star. Her name was Brenda Tarpley. I was in the same grade with her sister, Linda. I used to watch Brenda and her mother walk past my house as they headed for the bus to Atlanta to appear on live TV on Saturday afternoons. She could belt out a song even in the third grade, which is where I first heard her sing. Red Foley discovered her and she moved to Nashville. She has become a legend in pop and country western music. Her name? Brenda Lee!

Backstage at the Grand Ole Opry, I roamed around. I was curious to see what I might find. I discovered the door of Roy Acuff's dressing room. I knew Roy Acuff was the real power behind the show's great success. Literally and figuratively, performers had to get past Acuff's door in order to get on stage! What caught my eyes that day, however, was the inscription beneath Roy Acuff's name: "There ain't nothing gonna come up today that me and the Lord can't handle."

■　■　■

> "I have been down many times to my knees
> by the overwhelming conviction
> that I had nowhere to go but prayer.
> My own conclusion was that all about me
> seemed insufficient for the day."
>
> —Abraham Lincoln

Those words grabbed me. It sounded a lot like a country and western song. However you say it, though, the meaning is the same. When we run out of strength, the Lord will carry us on His shoulders.

There's a memorable poem about this extra power in our lives. It was written by Mary Stevenson after she experienced a powerful dream.

One night a man had a dream. He
dreamed he was walking along the beach
with the Lord. Across the sky flashed scenes
from his life. For each scene, he noticed two
sets of footprints in the sand; one belonged to
him, and the other to the Lord.

When the last scene in his life flashed
before him, he looked back at the footprints
in the sand. He noticed that many times

along the path of his life there was only one
set of footprints. He also noticed that it
happened at the very lowest and saddest
times in his life.

This really bothered him and he questioned
the Lord about it. "Lord, You said that once
I decided to follow You, You'd walk with me
all the way. But I have noticed that during
the most troublesome times in my life, there
is only one set of footprints. I don't
understand why when I needed You most You
would leave me."

The Lord replied, "My son, My precious
child, I love you and would never leave you.
During your times of trial and suffering,
When you see only one set of footprints,
It was then that I carried you."[5]

LET GOD WORK OUT THINGS

It's comforting to know that I'm not in the business of life
by myself. It's reassuring to believe that when we run out of
strength, the Lord will carry us on His shoulders. When I
approach life with that attitude—when I let God work out
things—my *can'ts* become transformed into *cans*, my *disabilities*

into *possibilities*, my *scars* into *stars*. Life opens up. Doors that close lead to bigger doors that open.

■   ■   ■

A very talented Englishman experienced so many setbacks and tragedies that he set out to take his own life. He dressed himself carefully, walked out of his apartment onto a London street on a dismal, foggy day, and hailed a horse-drawn taxi. "London Bridge," he instructed the driver. He meant to jump from the bridge and end his grief.

The fog was so thick, however, that horse and driver became lost. When the horse at last plodded to a stop, the driver told his passenger he could go no further. The man disembarked and when he got his bearings, he was shocked to find himself not at the London Bridge but back at his own doorstep.

William Cowper stumbled back into his little apartment and went into deep thought. At last he seated himself at his desk and penned these now-famous lines:

> God moves in a mysterious way
> His wonders to perform;
> He plants His footsteps in the sea,
> And rides upon the storm.

Deep in unfathomable mines
Of never-failing skill
He treasures up his bright designs,
And works his sovereign will.

Ye fearful saints, fresh courage take,
The clouds ye so much dread
Are big with mercy, and shall break
In blessings on your head.

Judge not the Lord by feeble-sense
But trust Him for His grace;
Behind a frowning providence
He hides a smiling face.

His purposes will ripen fast,
Unfolding every hour;
The bud may have a bitter taste,
But sweet will be the flower.

Blind unbelief is sure to err,
And scan his work in vain:
God is his own interpreter,
And he will make it plain.[6]

A great Atlanta jazz musician, Thomas Dorsey, wrote a gospel song entitled "Precious Lord, Take My Hand." It was written after Dorsey's pregnant wife died suddenly. He experienced a crisis of faith that shook him to his roots.

In the midst of his agony, Mr. Dorsey wrote the following lyrics:

Precious Lord, take my hand,

Lead me on, let me stand,

I am tired, I am weak, I am worn,

Through the storm, through the night,

Lead me on to the light,

Take my hand, precious Lord, lead me home.[7]

I've learned to reach out and ask the Lord to take my hand, to lead me on, and let me stand.

A SPIRITUAL FORCE MIGHTIER THAN ANY OTHER

It helps to know that when things go wrong, God still works in mysterious ways. Whether or not we recognize it, the awesome power of God has worked in our lives from the beginning of our lives. This power is available to us at any

> *"Great men are they who see the spiritual force is stronger than any material force, and that thought rules the world."*
>
> —*Ralph Waldo Emerson*

moment throughout our lives. Although I don't know why trials come, I believe this: We never walk through them alone. It's been my experience that the Lord walks with us and leads us on to higher

> *The Lord stood with me and strengthened me.*
> —2 Timothy 4:17a

ground. I've learned to trust the truth: "There ain't nothing gonna come up today that me and the Lord can't handle!"

Dr. Lloyd Ogilvie has a contemporary version of the Twenty-third Psalm that I like:

> The Lord is my strength, I shall not panic;
> He helps me relax and rest in quiet trust.
> He reminds me that I belong to Him
> And restores my serenity;
> He leads me in my decisions and
> Gives me calmness of mind.
> His presence is peace
> Even though I walk through the valley
> Of fear of failure,
> I will not worry, for he will be with me.
> His truth, grace, and loving kindness
> Will stabilize me.
> He prepares release and renewal in
> The midst of my stress.
> He anoints my mind with wisdom;

My cup overflows with fresh energy
Surely goodness and mercy will be
Communicated through me,
For I shall walk in the strength of my Lord,
And dwell in His presence forever.
Amen[8]

We can go for the max if we let God work out things in our lives.

10

SUCCESS IS A TEAM EFFORT

"Coming together is a beginning;
Keeping together is progress,
Working together is success."

—*Henry Ford*

A simple but stunning event recently made everything I've always believed about teamwork hit home.

It all began in my Senate office, with a name on a list of telephone calls. As I dialed David Lloyd's number, I had no idea who he might be or how I could help him. Within seconds, I realized that this was not a normal conversation with a constituent. He was going to help me!

Lloyd, a former United States Marine corporal, identified himself as the first to reach me after the grenade explosion which took my legs and my right arm. He had seen a television program about medics in which I had related details of that event and my account of the medics who saved my life. I had told of jumping from a helicopter, seeing a grenade lying on the ground, and concluding it had dropped from my web gear. I had reached for it . . . .

Now, nearly thirty-one years after that April 8, 1968, episode near Khe Sanh, Vietnam, David Lloyd was on the phone filling me in on details of those first moments when the grenade went off. A young soldier, new to the war, just behind me as we exited the helicopter, had straightened out the pins on his grenades to make them easier to pull in combat. The grenade had fallen off *his* web gear, *not mine*. Lloyd told about dressing the soldier's multiple shrapnel wounds—"maybe twenty-five battle dressings, the most I ever applied to one man"—while the soldier sobbed uncontrollably, not from pain but from anguish.

"It was my grenade, it was my grenade," he wept.

■ ■ ■

I was shocked. I quickly arranged for David and his wife, Mimi, a medical doctor, to meet me for lunch. There I learned more about the experience that had changed my life.

Everything came rushing back in vivid detail. Powerful emotions swept over me during Lloyd's account and pervaded my thoughts in the following weeks. As journalist David Pace wrote in a story for Associated Press:

> "I couldn't believe it," said Cleland. "For thirty-one years you have in your mind a certain set of circumstances that you've pretty much come to terms with and all of a sudden a call like this out of the blue changes everything for you. . . . It sent cold chills down my spine, caused me to relive the whole thing."

PRACTICING GOOD TEAMWORK

One of the most powerful recollections Lloyd's visit kindled in me was memories of battlefield teamwork. Our lives in Vietnam depended on how well we functioned *as a team.* The young soldier who made the tragic mistake was no less a team player than I or anyone else. The mishap could have happened to anyone. There were hundreds of moments in Vietnam when any one of us could have intersected with tragedy, at any time and at any place.

Military teamwork saves lives, and I owe *my* life to that fact. David Lloyd described how he rushed toward me

> *"A team exists only when each player*
> *understands how his actions affect*
> *the rest of the team."*
>
> —*Anonymous*

following the explosion, pulling off his web gear to make me a tourniquet, and cutting away my uniform to stop the bleeding. My legs were smoking, Lloyd said. I actually remember someone cutting off my uniform before I was rushed to the nearest aid station, where other teams worked furiously to save my life. Only someone like David Lloyd could have known that fact.

Memories of the various teams who worked on me near Khe Sanh, in the evacuation helicopter, in the hospitals in Vietnam, in the hospitals in Japan, in the Walter Reed Army Hospital in Washington, D.C.—and later, the rehabilitation teams at the Veterans Administration hospital—remain quite clear. More than ever, now, I realize that my life was saved on the battlefield by the grace of God and dozens of individuals who came to my aid, both then and afterward.

NO ONE SUCCEEDS ALONE

David's visit began a chain of recollections and realizations, not just about wartime events, but about how much teamwork went into the making of my life. Whatever success I have attained, I realize, has resulted from the efforts of count-less others!

First, I am convinced that the Lord has led me in His foot-prints throughout my life . . . and has carried me many times, though I did not know it and I did not acknowledge it!

I have also received much help from family and friends. Mark Twain once observed that the best thing a young person could do is choose the right parents. I followed that advice and chose very well. Hugh and Juanita Cleland not only were responsible for bringing me into this world, but also for raising me in this world. As we say in the South, "They done good."

If I turned out well, my parents are the ones who deserve the credit. Many other family members deserve appreciation as well. Although I was an only child, I was brought up in a won-derful extended family. Both of my parents had numerous brothers and sisters, and I was blessed with many cousins. And though my grandfathers died before I was born, I received a special blessing in my grandmothers.

In short, I had "good raisin'." I lacked for nothing. Looking back, I realize I am the product of a large team of people who from the earliest days of my life helped me achieve success. I had great teachers in my elementary school and high school, and Mr. W. L. Colombo, my principal throughout my twelve-year school career, was a magnificent role model.

Hillary Rodham Clinton has made one African proverb especially famous: "It takes a village to raise a child." That's certainly true in my case. The entire "village" of Lithonia, Georgia, raised me. During the early 1980s, our "village" decided to honor singer Brenda Lee and me by naming streets for us. Brenda's street is "Brenda Lee Lane"; mine is called "Max Cleland Boulevard."

"My" street goes through the center of downtown Lithonia, where I once ran barefooted in the summer, went to cowboy movies on Saturdays, and held my first job. Max Cleland Boulevard really should be named for all those good people who helped me along the way. I wish I could put the name of every one of them on that street sign. They belong there.

> *"We all of us tend to rise or fall together."*
> —*Theodore Roosevelt*

ACKNOWLEDGE OTHERS

Teamwork *saved* my life, and great teamwork also *built* my life. Looking back, however, I can see how self-centered I've been so much of the time. I regret that. I wish I had given more credit to the hard work and good example of my family, parents, schoolmates, teachers, and teammates.

Then there are the voters who helped put me in public office. Had it not been for *thousands* of voters in DeKalb County where I grew up, I would never have been elected to my first political office, the Georgia State Senate.

Had it not been for *hundreds of thousands* of Georgia voters statewide, I would not have been elected Georgia's Secretary of State.

Had it not been for the graciousness and confidence of two key people in Washington during the 1970s—President Jimmy Carter and Senator Alan Cranston, then chairman of the U.S. Senate Veterans Affairs Committee—I would not have been head of the Veterans Administration.

And certainly, had it not been for more than *1.2 million citizens* on election day, November 5, 1996, I would never have had the chance to serve in the United States Senate. I realize, now, how much my success in life has had to do with others who helped me succeed. Former Georgia governor Zell Miller used to say, "When you see a turtle on a fence post, you realize it didn't get there by itself." I didn't get where I am by myself. It was a team effort. I keep a turtle on a fence post on my desk in my Atlanta office to remind me of that fact. It was given to me by friends who helped put me in that office!

BECOMING A STRONG TEAM PLAYER

In the world of professional basketball, Michael Jordan is considered one of the greatest basketball players ever to explode across the court. Not only was Jordon great, but his presence galvanized his team to greatness as well. He led by example. As a kid, though, Jordan was cut from his eighth-grade basketball team. He decided to bounce back by practicing harder and working harder than the rest. Today, he is celebrated as a magnificent, record-breaking athlete and a team player.

Pat Riley, former coach of the Los Angeles Lakers, relates a marvelous story about another great basketball player in his book, *The Winner Within.* Riley describes one young kid who obviously was a basketball superstar from day one. During his early years, a coach had instructed the youngster, "You're the best we've got. When you get the ball, shoot it!"

From that day on, the young man did exactly as the coach told him. He got the ball. He dribbled down court. He found a place to pivot, jump, and shoot. Swish! Two points! He dazzled everyone who watched him play.

Time after time, the star player made his team victorious. They won championships. They were lauded as outstanding. However, the young man soon noticed that while the press and fans proclaimed him as a hero game after game, other players walked off the court shaking their heads. They felt left out. They did not share in the glory. It did not seem like *their* victory.

At that point, Coach Riley says, the legendary record-breaking team of the Los Angeles Lakers during the 1980s was born. While still in college, the emerging star had decided he would change his game and always share his amazing prowess with his teammates. Whenever he went in for a score, he would pass the ball and allow a teammate to dunk it. He led his team in *scoring*. He also led his team in *assists*.

This became a trend he continued throughout his basketball career. When he entered the N.B.A. as a young superstar drafted by the Lakers as their leading point guard, he brought magic to the team. The young kid indeed was "magic"—Earvin "Magic" Johnson.

Not only did Magic Johnson become a spectacular superstar who led the Lakers to world records, but he had the ability to make his *teammates* perform and feel like superstars. His team-work, as much as his own performance, became a special inspiration to millions around the world. After being diagnosed as HIV-positive during the early 1990s, Johnson retired from professional basketball, only to make a dramatic comeback in 1996 as the Lakers' coach, as he continued to battle against the odds.

Again he encouraged his team. He lifted their performance and inspired the nation. Magic Johnson represents to me someone who is a devoted team player.

GIVE MORE CREDIT AND RESPECT

I love any story about Casey Stengel, coach of the New York Yankees during their glory days of the 1950s. However, in Stengel's last year as a professional baseball manager, he had a new team—the New York Mets. It was their first year as a team.

The players for the Mets seemed far from promising. The legendary coach quickly became frustrated by all the dropped balls in the outfield. He criticized the young men when they missed the steal sign from third base. He became outraged by their poor hitting. The pitching was terrible.

One day Casey shouted out to nobody in particular, "Does anybody here know how to play this game?"

At season's end, Stengal called the team together. The novice group had finished last in the league. Stengal noted that they had been through a tough year, but he urged them not to become discouraged. In his inimitable style, he attempted to comfort the young men about their poor season, ending with these words: "Don't worry, boys. It was a team effort all the way!"

Teams can accomplish miracles when individuals fail. As Daniel Webster once wrote,

> Men do jointly what they cannot do singly;
> and the union of minds and hands, the
> concentration of their power,
> becomes almost omnipotent.

We can go for the max in life if we commit ourselves to making success a team effort!

"A good manager is one who can get twenty-five guys to play for the name on the front of their shirt and not the name on the back of their shirt."

—*Tommy LaSorda*

11

BE OF
GOOD
COURAGE

"Courage is doing what you're afraid to do.
There is no courage unless you're scared."
—*Captain Eddie Rickenbacker*

A minister friend of mine once took a trip to London. While traveling about the city, he saw numerous billboards which trumpeted the slogan, "Have Courage." He thought to himself, *These British people are tough. They still have the spirit of surviving the Battle of Britain and the Blitz in World War II.* One week later, he discovered Courage was the name of a beer.

I've discovered that courage does not come from some substance outside your body but that it is something discovered deep within your soul.

Dr. Norman Vincent Peale once told of visiting Switzerland and standing at the base of the great mountain peak known as the Matterhorn. As he gazed at the massive edifice, he spotted from the corner of his eye a small cemetery nestled in the shadows near the base.

Curious as always, Dr. Peale explored the cemetery. He came across a stone which bore a fascinating inscription: "We who lie here scorned the lesser peaks."

The first thing I learned about living life to the fullest and going for the max was that it takes courage. Certainly it takes courage to "scorn the lesser peaks" and climb toward higher levels of strength and success. I believe that finding the courage to move onward and upward may be the toughest challenge any of us ever faces. Yet, it's the most rewarding.

Woody Allen has a funny line. He says his goal in life is to "climb a low mountain." Many people like that idea because climbing low mountains seems easy. It's not much of a challenge. Actually, most of us set far lower standards for ourselves than we know we are capable of achieving. Allen also quips, "Ninety percent of

> *"One man with courage makes a majority."*
> —Andrew Jackson

life is showing up." I've been grateful some days just to show up. But, that's not *all* I want in life. I prefer to find the courage to do more.

A generation ago, an American lady with a modest personality taught herself to overcome her shyness and trepidation. She eventually became one of our nation's boldest, most eloquent speakers on behalf of the less fortunate.

Eleanor Roosevelt, in confessing her early fears about speaking in public, offered a prescription for courage:

> Fear is the most devastating emotion on earth. I conquered it by helping those who were worse off than I was. I believe that anyone can conquer fear by doing the things he fears to do, provided he keeps doing them until he gets a record of successful experiences behind him!

■　■　■

Before Vietnam, I had a very superficial understanding of courage. After completing Army paratrooper school, I thought I was God's gift to the army. I possessed the classic paratrooper's view on courage. I thought courage was the *absence* of fear.

Then I got to Vietnam. I got shot at, rocketed, mortared, and attacked. During combat, I experienced sheer terror. The total, stark fear I experienced in Vietnam felt like nothing I had known before, and nothing I have known since.

Because I experienced such utter, gripping fear, I believed I had lost my courage. I went to my superior officer and confessed my fears. We were engaged in the largest helicopter combat assault of the Vietnam War, the relief of the siege of Khe Sanh. I surely did not feel heroic.

> "What time I am afraid, I will trust in thee."
>
> —Psalm 56:3

"That's all right, " Major Maury Cralle reassured me. "Just keep your mind on your job and you'll be fine." I believed him. Major Cralle, a West Point graduate, already had won two Silver Stars in combat. If anyone knew anything about the courage to overcome fear, I reasoned, it would be Maury Cralle.

Ernest Hemingway once described courage as "grace under pressure." General Omar Bradley, the great World War II commander, said courage is the ability to do your job while you're "half scared to death." I have been half scared to death many times. Later, back in the states, I read a sign on a church bulletin board which helped my thinking: "Courage is fear which has said its prayers."

I like that. I have learned that the presence of fear does not mean the absence of courage. Courage is saying our prayers and pressing on.

In Vietnam, I learned I never wanted to be with those who were *not* scared. If they were not scared, I reasoned, they didn't fully comprehend what was going on. Recently, reporters asked a Spanish astronaut, one of the crew members on the space shuttle flight carrying Senator John Glenn, if he was scared. He replied that he felt like the bullfighters in Spain. If you are not afraid of the bull, you don't understand the situation.

COURAGE TO GO FOR THE MAX

We who would have it all must risk it all. Jesus said we must lose our life in order to save it. And so it is. We cannot accomplish what we need to accomplish unless we step forward in courage.

Attila the Hun stated, "You can't lead the army from the rear chariot." Similarly, General George S. Patton, Jr. declared that you can't make a good battlefield decision from an armchair. If we're going to make good decisions about life, we must get into life and get a feel for it. We must find the courage to take the lead chariot. We don't experience the highest and best life can offer by deciding to climb only the low mountains.

Kim Basinger, the Academy-Award-winning actress and Georgia native, said, "I don't want to just survive; I want to thrive." My sentiments exactly. And I've learned I must become

> *"The brave are surely those who have the clearest vision of what is before them, glory and danger alike, and yet go out to meet it."*
>
> —*Pericles*

brave enough to climb the highest peaks if I'm to live life to the fullest and go for the max!

Courage can lead to a fuller life. Professor Sidney Hood put it this way: "My observations lead me to the conclusion that human beings have suffered greater deprivation from their fear of life than from its abundance."

■ ■ ■

Major Cralle's lesson about handling one's fear continues in my life to this day. I have learned that despite any feelings of lack of courage, it is possible to focus on today's job and accomplish it. In fearful times, when I blot out all distractions, erase yesterday and tomorrow, and focus on today, I can find the courage to do what I need to do.

Courage consists of putting one foot in front of the other and moving forward. When I fail to do this, I lose my focus. I no longer can live life to the max. But when I determine to summon enough courage to put one foot in front of the other, so to speak, wonderful things open up in my life. Even a thimbleful of courage creates energy to press on.

Franklin D. Roosevelt offered us a profound Depression-era truth that works. He said in 1933, "The only thing we have to fear is fear itself!" As Sir Edmund Hillary so aptly put it after becoming the first man to scale Mt. Everest, "It is not the mountain we conquer, but ourselves."

Conquering fear, for me, has been a big mountain to climb. Mostly, it involves conquering myself. I have learned that I can conquer the mountain of fear that often looms within me. But it takes courage.

I believe the Lord gives us the courage to meet the challenges of each day. The Bible tells us we were created only "a little lower than the angels" (Ps. 8:5). Dr. Lloyd Ogilvie translates this to mean, "a little lower than Himself." We were created, therefore, to live life at the higher peaks, close to God, and He gives us the courage to do it!

In President John F. Kennedy's book, *Profiles in Courage*, he observes that for courage, "Each man has to look within his own soul." Indeed, the root word for *courage* comes from the Latin word meaning "heart." The Bible indicates as much. The Old Testament psalmist tells us, "Be of good courage, and He shall strengthen thine heart" (Ps. 27:14).

The more courage we exhibit, the more we acquire. The more "heart" we have for life, the more strength we develop to live it. These words of Thomas Edison challenge me:

My message to you is:

Be courageous! . . .

Be as brave as your fathers before you.

Have faith. Go forward.

SUCCESS REQUIRES COURAGE

Courage becomes a necessary ingredient if we mean to live our lives to the fullest. Henry David Thoreau tells in his classic work, *Walden,* that he decided to live "deliberately" or else risk "not having lived." At Walden Pond he discovered, "It's life nearest the bone that's the sweetest." It takes courage to experience life "nearest the bone," but I can testify that it's there that life is the sweetest.

I have visited the historic battlefield in Belgium where the Duke of Wellington defeated Napoleon in the early part of the nineteenth century. I also saw the house in which Wellington spent the night before that great battle.

History reports that Wellington got little sleep that night. He had a queasy stomach. I have had such feelings before a battle. The worst stress and pressure is *before* the battle, not *during* the battle. Wellington felt all those fears.

However, the next day he defeated Napoleon and changed the course of European history. When someone later asked the Duke what it took to win, he replied: "Three-o'clock-in-the-morning courage."

I have found it so in my life. When I come to the end of myself, I have one more place to go—to my knees in prayer for encouragement, strength, guidance, and fellowship with my Creator. I have learned that prayer—sometimes at three o'clock in the morning—enables me to regain the courage and confidence I need to live life "nearest the bone," and experience life in all its sweetness. Through prayer, God strengthens my heart and gives me courage.

Hank Viscanti, a friend from New York state, was born without legs. He dedicated his life to training the disabled. Hank believes this:

> There's a time to go to your knees in prayer,
> even those of us who have no knees. But there
> is also a time to get up off your knees,
> even those of us who have no knees.

To transform fear into courage, go to your knees in prayer, then get up off your knees in confidence that where the Lord leads, He will also provide protection and strength to go. As the psalmist assures us, "He that dwelleth in the secret place of the most High shall abide under the shadow of the Almighty" (Ps. 91:1).

Courage moves us forward in life, both as individuals and as nations. Arnold Toynbee, the great British historian, studied the rise and fall of twenty-six civilizations. He concluded that it was not the *challenge* to a civilization that determined its future, but its *response* to that challenge. So it is with each of us.

Another British writer, Aldous Huxley, summed it up: "Experience is not what happens to a man; it's what a man does with what happens to him."

"Do the thing you fear," Ralph Waldo Emerson advised, "and the death of fear is certain." Most assuredly, we can live life to the fullest and go for the max, but we must have the courage to overcome our fears, in order to fully embrace the opportunities before us.

12

ENJOY ALL THINGS

"I asked for all things that I might enjoy life.
I was given life that I might enjoy all things."
　　　　—A prayer of an unknown Confederate soldier

At a particularly depressing time in my life in 1973, I came across a marvelous personal inspiration. It was a prayer. It was given to me by a just-returned POW from the Vietnam War, Colonel Quincy Collins, from Charlotte, North Carolina. Colonel Collins, an Air Force pilot, had been shot down over North Vietnam. He had been held in captivity by the North Vietnamese for almost seven years. Much of that time he was held in solitary confinement. Colonel Collins spoke to a group of veterans in Georgia upon his return to the States. I was fortunate to be in the audience!

I was still struggling with my own reactions to the war when Colonel Collins recited in his closing remarks what he described as a "prayer of an unknown Confederate sol-

> *"Too much of a good thing is absolutely wonderful."*
>
> —Mae West

dier." Apparently, the prayer was so named because it had been discovered in a house in South Carolina after the Civil War. When the prayer got to a particular passage, I was struck by the phrase, "I asked for all things that I might enjoy life; I was given life that I might enjoy all things."

All of a sudden it hit me. I was alive! I had survived the horror of war. For what, I was not sure. But the one thing I did know was I was alive to now enjoy all of life.

I have treasured that poem ever since. Since then, I've tried

> *"We cannot take ourselves seriously if*
> *we cannot take ourselves lightly."*
> —*Dr. Harold E. Kohn*

to make the most of my life in every way and relish the efforts of all those who try to do the same.

One such individual is a personal friend, Joey Reiman. Joey is an Atlanta advertising and marketing genius. He stays so charged up that he makes the Energizer Bunny look like a couch potato. Joey has a slogan, however, which reminds him and his staff to stop and enjoy their lives: "Even the best have to rest."

According to Joey, time off does not equate to idleness, though. It's a way for the highly motivated and highly creative individual to stop, think, reflect, recharge the batteries, and refresh the spirit.

The Reiman agency's staff, in another idea from their endlessly creative chief, takes a day off each year on the fourth of March. March *Forth* is the idea. Everyone who works for Joey sets aside that day to "march forth" to promising new goals and objectives in their lives.

We all need such times. Most of us understand "burnout"; far fewer understand that "even the best have to rest." I must remind myself often that if I put down the shovel and stop digging, the world, as the *Desiderata* puts it so well, will "go on unfolding as it should," even without my tinkering with it.

LIVE THE EXPERIENCE

My father gardens. Among all the plants he grows each year, his tomato crop tops the rest. Before the ground warms each spring, he starts his seedlings indoors. From those flat yellow seeds will come the six-inch plants he'll set out in late March or early April. By July he'll harvest his first prize, and from then until frost those husky, staked branches will be heavy with fruit.

We'll enjoy those big, juicy tomatoes, fresh off the vine, all summer long. My father's tomatoes are summer to me. There's nothing in this world that tastes better than a tomato sand-wich—just bread, mayo, salt, pepper, and thick slices of ruby red tomato. That's living!

We all get a kick out of my lifelong appreciation for Daddy's tomatoes and Mother's sandwiches. While visiting my parents not long ago, I wheeled into the kitchen one morning with a good old tomato sandwich on my mind. Mother laughed and said, "This early? Heavens, I haven't even had my second cup of coffee!"

> *"If the day and the night are such that you greet them with joy, and life emits a fragrance like flowers and sweet-scented herbs, is more elastic, more starry, more immortal – that is your success."*
>
> —*Henry David Thoreau*

Live the experience, I say. My father's tomatoes, so much a part of every summer, remind us that life simply cannot be hurried. I gave Daddy a rock for his tomato bed, with the inscription: "The key to ripe tomatoes is to take a vacation." Sometimes it helps to let things just ripen in the sun.

HUMAN "DOING" OR HUMAN BEING?

For us workaholics who are always trying to tie up life's loose ends and drive hard to complete our various projects, it's easy to overlook the fun in life. We often forget to enjoy our victories. We miss out on *living* each experience.

We become what psychologist Dr. John Bradshaw, author and P.B.S. television star, calls "human *doings*" instead of "human *beings*." We forget to be!

Admittedly, I'm the chief among such sinners. My workaholic personality enjoys *doing*—campaigning, traveling, speaking, writing—rather than *being*. Striving toward a goal, fighting to survive, living life to the fullest, becoming strong at the broken places—all those things actually seem natural to me. These are things I have done all my life.

After I was wounded in Vietnam, this innate sense of urgency helped me deal positively with disabilities which could have been my undoing. What is hard for me, however, is not the *doing*, but the *being*.

As a leader, I can become so used to directing and even controlling people, events, and situations that I find it difficult to *follow*—whether in God's footprints or someone else's. I'm always *leading*. As natural as that seems, and as much as I enjoy it, it's hard to remember to stop and smell the roses. And as much as I love the scenery, I'm too often guilty of not enjoying it as I go by.

I'm inspired by the thought that whenever India's Mahatma Ghandi became most stressed, when he was most pressed by his people to "do something," he purposely slowed himself down. He fasted. He meditated. Ghandi once claimed, "There is more to life than increasing its speed!"

Lao-tzu, the Chinese philosopher, offered wise advice to those who would lead. Lao-tzu observed that the lowest level of leadership was the leader people *feared*. The next highest level was the leader people *loved*. However, according to Lao-tzu, the highest level belonged to the leader who created such a positive and constructive climate that when the work was done the people said, "We did it ourselves."

Those of us who would lead others to greatness, and would become great ourselves, should realize that in our democratic society our greatest goals are always achieved whenever our people can say, "We did it ourselves."

Victories in life, I remind myself, are to be enjoyed, not endured. We should learn to enjoy each victory we earn, and take time to soak up its meaning.

The Jewish and Christian faiths, with all other major religions of the world, have one day each week set aside as a holy day. This special day is one in which we dwell on the goodness of our Creator, enjoy and celebrate our lives, and return to wholeness. In Africa, they say that special day is for the purpose of "letting our souls catch up with our bodies."

> *"If you foolishly ignore beauty, your life will be impoverished."*
> —*Frank Lloyd Wright*

I continue to learn lessons which can come only from deliberately feeding the soul and spirit. Although this is difficult for a personality like mine, I am learning to just *be!*

From such fresh perspectives, I am learning how to truly enjoy each victory in my life. I realize how many broken places I have suffered. I think for that reason I am learning to enjoy more what I *have* rather than wasting time in regret over what I am *missing.*

SOMETHING YET TO DO

I believe the Lord has more victories in store for me than I can count! I really believe I'm just beginning to enjoy life now. It's great to have something to look forward to, to enjoy. As Viktor Frankl once pointed out, "It is always important to have something yet to do in life."

I have new challenges to meet, new peaks to climb, new valleys to walk through . . . and new worlds to conquer! Life

> *"Life for all its incompleteness*
> *is rather fun, sometimes."*
>
> —*Sir Winston Churchill*

for me is a constant series of challenges and opportunities to live a fuller life and go for the max in every way.

Alexander the Great, who had conquered the known world by age thirty-two, wept because he had no more worlds to conquer. I don't have that problem. There are worlds to conquer, and I know I must never stop using my talents and persistence in discovering them.

I believe that is true for all of us. We are designed and built to become world conquerors. We are destined to overcome obstacles. We are created to become trailblazers. We are programmed to explore and discover the universe around us and the Spirit within us. Eleanor Roosevelt believed that. She once wrote:

> You have to accept whatever comes,
> and the only important question is
> that you meet it with courage
> and the best you have to give.
>
> There *is* something yet to do. *We must grow.*
> We must continue to set great, purposeful goals.
> We must plan our future and think positively about it.

We can decide to move forward with more strength, more confidence, and more ambition than ever before. We know how to live "deliberately," as Thoreau put it. We know how to enjoy life "nearest the bone," to appreciate that life which is sweetest.

ALIVE DAY

One of the ways I enjoy life is on April 8th each year. That date marks the anniversary of my fateful encounter at Khe Sanh. It's a grim anniversary, some would say. But with the help of a dear friend, Jim Mayer, my executive officer during the 1970s when I headed the V. A., I see that event as the day when, by the grace of God and the help of friends, I stayed alive. I borrowed Jim Mayer's title which celebrates the day he lost both legs in Vietnam. He calls it Alive Day. I call it Alive Day too. On that day each year I celebrate just being alive.

The first Alive Day celebration I attended was for Jim. He hosted a group of us at dinner in an old Chesapeake Bay restaurant. That evening we stuffed ourselves with the finest local oysters and crabs, laughed, joked, and had a wonderful time. That's when I decided to do exactly what Jim had done—turn an otherwise dreaded anniversary into an event that celebrates life.

Alive Day gets better every year. It's a time I look forward to with great excitement. I put a lot of thought and planning it. My list of invitees grows larger every year. It's a day for positive thinking, pure enjoyment, and appreciating those who put extra life into my living year after year.

It would be hard to top my thirtieth annual celebration, I thought, because my senatorial duties took me to Europe during that week for some awesome and exciting events. I'll never forget watching some of the troops in training as medics in Germany . . . the reception for us at Ramstein Air Force Base . . . then flying to Bosnia to visit American troops.

That Alive Day was filled with pride in America and gratitude for all it stands for. Other Alive Day events have included a fishing trip with my father, a fund-raising event for my next political race, dinner with a few close friends—or a few hundred—and messages from friends, along with fun, happiness, and surprises.

One of the best things about Alive Day is the way it spills over into the lives of others. Janet Powell, an attorney for a North Carolina utilities company, was living in Atlanta when we met five years ago. I introduced her to the Alive Day concept during a poignant conversation.

■　■　■

Janet and I met on a Saturday afternoon shortly after what she calls the worst happening in her life. Two weeks earlier, she had been raped—the final victim of a rapist in a months-long series of assaults in her upscale Atlanta neighborhood.

Her physical bruises were mostly healed, but she was still suffering emotionally. That afternoon she decided to visit a friend who lives in the same Atlanta apartment building where I live. Jan and her friend intended to have a real "pity party."

Jan was waiting in the lobby for an elevator when I came into the building. I asked her who she was visiting. When she told me, I replied, "I know her. I think I'll go up with you and say hello!" The afternoon turned into a time of good conversation, jokes, and lots of laughter.

Afterwards, I suggested we go out for dinner. During our conversation, I asked, "Did you read about that guy? The one they finally caught?"

Jan appeared to go into shock. We had not mentioned the assaults. She knew I didn't know about her experience. She looked down at the table, obviously shaken.

"Are you all right?" I asked. Jan nodded her head.

"Are you sure you're all right?" I asked again.

At last she swallowed and said, "I was the woman."

It was a shocking moment. I leaned toward Jan, took her hand, and asked, "Do you remember the date when it happened?"

"Max, I will *always* remember that date," she said, with irony in her voice.

"Jan, for the rest of your life, that will be your Alive Day," I told her. I went on to explain that she must celebrate the fact that she was nearly killed, but had been spared. *She had been given life to enjoy all things.*

■ ■ ■

Alive Day helped Jan shift her perspective from deep grief to gratitude. She has since told her story—one that brings tears to every eye—to groups of people who need to hear her positive message. A faith-filled woman, Janet Powell exudes life and health. Her Alive Day has helped turn her scars into stars.

■   ■   ■

To focus on Alive Day, to concentrate on having fun, also reminds me not to take life too seriously. I remember the last time I saw the late U.S. Senator Richard Russell, Georgia's powerful elder statesman, in his Washington, D.C. office. It was December of 1969.

With pride, I approached the great man on my new artificial limbs.

"What are you going to do with yourself now, young man?" he asked in his penetrating way. I knew this was more than just small talk.

"Sir, I'm going back to Georgia and I'm thinking of going into politics."

"Good," Senator Russell replied. "Just remember, always take your job seriously, but not yourself." It's the best political advice I've ever received. Alive Day helps me take my job seriously, but not myself.

■ ■ ■

Alive Day helped Jim Mayer, Janet Powell, and me turn our lives around. Each year, as we go for the max, we add more benefits and blessings that are reasons for celebration. This year, my thirty-first Alive Day, we packed out the Officers' Club at Fort McPherson, just outside Atlanta, for an occasion to remember. Every Alive Day is different, but this time we added a new feature; the first annual Max Cleland Alive Day award.

We flew David Lloyd and his wife, Dr. Mimi Lloyd, to Atlanta for the event. Amid a time of lively tributes, jokes, and fun, we presented the plaque to David for helping keep me alive thirty-one years ago on the battlefield.

That small trophy was a tiny symbol which represents all those who have impacted my life. I celebrate each of these lives every time I celebrate my own Alive Day.

The following day I participated in the ceremony for an Atlanta neighborhood which was celebrating its reconstruction after a terrible tornado a year earlier. *This community is celebrating its own Alive Day*, I thought.

A policeman approached me. "Sir, I saw your Alive Day on the news last night. From now on I'll celebrate my own Alive Day on the anniversary of the day I got shot!"

We should learn to make every day a day in which we celebrate being alive. We are blessed. We can go for the max and live life to the fullest. We can enjoy all things because we are alive!

I asked God for strength, that I might achieve;
I was made weak, that I might learn humbly to obey.
I asked for health, that I might do greater things;
I was given infirmity that I might do better things.
I asked for riches, that I might be happy;
I was given poverty, that I might be wise.
I asked for power, that I might have the praise of men;
I was given weakness, that I might feel the need of
God.
I asked for all things, that I might enjoy life;
I was given life, that I might enjoy all things.
I got nothing that I asked for—but everything I
had hoped for.
Almost despite myself, my unspoken prayers were
answered.
I among all men, am most richly blessed.
—A prayer of an unknown Confederate soldier

CONCLUSION

"Life does not have to be perfect for it to be wonderful."

—*Annette Funicello*

Life," quipped the distinguished British Prime Minister Benjamin Disraeli, "is too short to be little."

Exactly!

We must make the most of it while we are alive! We must go for the max. I've discovered that Dr. Peale is right when he advises, "Never minimize yourself. Maximize yourself." I hope I can do that all the rest of my days.

I once asked my grandmother, whom I adored, what she thought about life. "Honey," she said, "it's the best thing I ever did." I love that. I want to make my life the best thing I've ever done. I hope you do too! That's why we should go for the max every way, every day.

> *Dance like nobody is watching,*
> *Love like you've never been hurt,*
> *Work like you're not being paid.""*
>
> —*Anonymous*

I love a poem by the Victorian poet, Alfred Lord Tennyson. The poem is entitled *Ulysses*. It paints the legendary Greek hero as a man of action anxious to get on with life and living. The poem concludes with words that inspire and strengthen my heart to continue to go for the max in my life:

Come, my friends.

'Tis not too late to seek a newer world.

Push off, and sitting well in order smite

The sounding furrows; for my purpose holds

To sail beyond the sunset, and the baths

Of all the Western stars, until I die.

It may be that the gulfs will wash us down;

It may be we shall touch the Happy Isles,

And see the great Achilles, whom we knew.

Tho' much is taken, much abides; and tho'

We are not now that strength which in old days

Moved earth and heaven; that which we are, we are—

One equal temper of heroic hearts,

Made weak by time and fate, but strong in will

To strive, to seek, to find, and not to yield.

ENDNOTES

1. Martin Luther King Jr., from a speech circa early 1960s.

2. Benjamin Mays, from a speech given during his tenure as president of Morehouse College, Atlanta, Georgia.

3. Dennis Kimbro, *Think and Grow Rich: A Black Choice* (New York: Ballantine Books, 1992), n.p.

4. Earl Nightingale, from a radio broadcast circa 1960s.

5. Mary Stevenson, "I Had a Dream" (also known as "Footprints in the Sand"), originally written in 1936, copyright 1984.

6. William Cowper, "Light Shining Out of Darkness," 1774.

7. "Take My Hand, Precious Lord" (a.k.a. "Precious Lord, Take My Hand") by Thomas A. Dorsey, © 1938 (Renewed) Warner-Tamerlane Publishing Corp. For the USA. All Rights for the World excluding USA controlled by Unichappell Music, Inc. All Right Reserved. Used by permission of Warner Bros. Publications U.S., Inc. Miami, Florida 33014.

8. Lloyd John Ogilvie, *One Quiet Moment* (Eugene, Ore.: Harvest House Publishers, 1977), February 10 entry.